THE PRIZE WINNERS HANDBOOK

By
Jeffrey Feinman

D1053844

CONTENTS

Chapter One

WHY I WROTE THIS BOOK

"Are those sweepstakes really legitimate?" It's a question that people ask me all the time. "Does someone really win the prizes?" Or, "Don't the prizes go to friends of the judging organization?"

Yes. Yes. No.

The great American dream has always been to strike it rich fast. That's the story of Columbus who, looking for spices and tea, accidentally found a continent. It's the story of the California Gold Rush that lured thousands of people westward to pan for gold. It's the story of the Texas oil wells. An accident. A miracle. A gushing black fountain in your own backyard. Somewhere each of us, deep in his heart of hearts, has the secret wish to become a millionaire.

But few of us know how to go about it.

Have you ever entered a contest or a sweepstakes?

5

Have you ever bought a chance in a lottery? Have you ever played bingo and won?

Maybe you have—once. Or twice. Or, maybe you've never entered at all, never tried your luck, never played to win.

There's the wonderful story of William Schaeffer, a bartender, who bought a ticket in a lottery and thought he was so stupid for wasting his money that he signed himself ";W. Dopie."

"For years," he said, "I bought losing tickets in the Sweepstakes. On this ticket I got as far as the "W" of my first name, and I said to myself, 'Ach, what a dope I am to waste the money,' and instead of my real name, I put down Dopie."

This ticket won him $50,000.

Along with the dream comes the suspicion, "Oh, I could never win." Or, "Why should I bother? Everybody knows those sweepstakes are a ripoff. Everybody knows you lose out. It's a waste of time. A waste of postage." Or, "They aren't legitimate. The winners are friends of the judges." Or, "Nobody wins. I never knew anybody to win. They never give away real prizes."

For the past ten years I have been involved in various aspects of the prize-promotion business. Currently. I'm president of Ventura Associates, a sales-promotion agency that conducts contests and sweepstakes for some of this country's largest advertisers. I wrote this book to answer your questions about prize promotions and lotteries, and to give you the information you need to win.

The truth is, you *can* win a sweepstakes. Thousands of people do. And sweepstakes *are* legitimate. And in the big, national contests, the winners are *never* friends of the judges.

This book will once and for all set the record straight.

It will show you a phenomenal opportunity to be part of the million-dollar giveaway. That's right. Each year in the United States millions of dollars in cash, houses, cars, and other merchandise are given away. Best of all, these prizes are given away to people just like you.

This book will tell you how you can get your fair share.

Types of Prize Promotions

Prize promotions fall into several distinct categories. Basically, these are lotteries, contests, sweepstakes, games and bingo.

A lottery has the elements of prize, chance, and consideration present. Lotteries are legal only when conducted by a state government. Usually, the prizes are monetary. Of course, the element of chance is the fact that you have a chance or opportunity to win. The consideration is the money that you spend to buy a lottery ticket.

There has been a tremendous growth in lotteries in the last decade. In the lottery section of this book, we will examine the reasons for this and how you can take part in this huge giveaway.

Lotteries are strictly illegal when run by companies. In order for a manufacturer to run a prize promotion, he must eliminate one of the elements of a lottery. In this way he changes its form and makes it legal.

Usually, a firm eliminates the element of consideration, and runs a prize promotion called a sweepstakes. The way the offer is conducted is simple.

There is a series of prizes offered and the consumer is invited to send in his name and address. The element of consideration is not present, because the consumer is not required to buy anything or send any money in order to enter.

In the case of a lottery, you must buy at least 1 ticket. The usual cost of a ticket is about 50 cents. The money collected from the tickets goes partly to pay for the prizes and partly to the state.

In a sweepstakes, the manufacturer makes no money directly. You don't have to pay to enter. All you have to pay is the postage.

You may be familiar with these sweepstakes. In some cases you are asked to send the label from a product or simply the name of the product printed on a 3"x5" card. Obviously the manufacturer would prefer that you buy the product, but he can't demand that you buy it. Your opportunity to win is not based on whether or not you purchase the product.

This is one of the reasons why many people are suspicious of sweepstakes. It's the old saying about something for nothing, but few people really believe they can win without effort.

You're already convinced that a company isn't going to give anything away free. Well, some companies do. They do it because there's something in it for them. And they do it because there's something in it for you. It turns out that this kind of prize promotion has something in it for everyone. I'll explain this later. For now, suffice it to say, you don't have to pay anything but the postage.

The other type of company prize promotion is a

contest of skill. Here the element of chance is not present. Again, this is what makes a contest different from a lottery. The missing element of chance makes a contest legal.

The very fact that skill is required obviously means that the element of chance has been removed. In this case, consideration may be present. The manufacturer may require you to buy a product as a requirement for entry. You have undoubtedly seen such contests advertised where you were required, say, to mail in 3 bottle labels along with the completion of a sentence such as "I like Hunter's catsup because . . . ," in 25 words or less.

Another type of prize promotion run by companies is commonly referred to as a game. These are offers in which you save or match pieces. They are usually associated with a prize promotion conducted in order to get you to enter a place of business.

The most common of these is the gas-station game conducted several years ago by major petroleum companies. The consumer was asked to save pieces of a game ticket and match the halves.

This type of game is also used by fast-food operations and supermarket chains.

Finally, an additional type of prize promotion quite common and very popular especially among older folk is bingo. Bingo games are usually run by religious or charitable organizations. In New York City there are actually special halls devoted to bingo. They are rented out by these organizations for a certain period of time, but most people who go to play bingo don't care in the least who's running the operation. They simply want to play and they simply want to win.

Chapter Fifteen on bingo explains how to increase your opportunity to win.

Why Do Companies Run Sweepstakes?

Each year, thousands upon thousands of people receive a letter that says, "Congratulations, you're the winner of a . . . prize offer." You've probably received such a letter in the mail at one time or another. And you've probably wanted to know why any company would want to do such a thing.

Why do companies run prize promotions? Why does the church run bingo games? Why do certain states run lotteries?

The answer in all cases is the same. To make money.

In the case of the lottery, this answer seems to make the most sense. You pay to enter a lottery. You pay for each chance you take, each ticket that you obtain. The state makes some 40 to 50 percent profit from each ticket. The rest of the money goes to pay for prizes.

If you play bingo, of course, you pay for the chance to win. Usually you must pay for each card that you buy. If you play one game and use 40 cards, you must pay for each of those 40 cards. Again, it's obvious how the church or other sponsoring organization makes money.

In the case of prize-promotion contests, it's also easy to see how the company makes money. Usually, in the contest you are required to save labels or boxtops. In other words, the promoters require that you buy their product. If you need three boxtops, you have to buy three boxes of so-and-so's ready-to-eat cereal. If you need soap wrappers, you have to buy bars of soap. It makes little difference to the manufacturer whether you buy the soap yourself or get your friends to buy the soap. The point is, you and others have bought it and will probably continue to buy the product.

But no doubt the free sweepstakes still leaves a rather large question in your mind. It's too much like the old American saying, "you don't get something for nothing." How can the manufacturer afford to give away prizes when he doesn't even request that you buy his product?

Well, indirectly he does. That's all any advertisement is—an indirect request to buy.

Major companies consider the price of sweepstakes prizes as simply another advertising cost. The sweepstakes is something like the brass band to attract attention to a product or service. American marketers have discovered that the chance of winning turns on consumers and creates a good deal of involvement and excitement. They have found that by running a sweepstakes offer in an ad that the advertising readership of that ad will increase. Everyone may be suspicious of getting something for nothing but secretly everyone wants to believe it. Everyone wants to be a winner. Everyone reads the ads that promise prizes.

One national magazine that runs sweepstakes feels that properly run promotions are as good for them as they are for their readers. They say that the sweepstakes is merely a device to attract attention to their magazine and the various other products they have to offer. For the reader, of course, there's the pleasure of playing the game and the possibility of winning many valuable prizes.

Many advertisers have found that storekeepers will devote space for big displays to promote a sweepstakes. This is good for both the storekeeper and the advertiser. Such a display draws customers into the store who will not only buy the product and thus help the advertiser, but will also buy many other products.

The sweepstakes is a great advertising tool, and it's good for you to know this, simply from the standpoint of being a potential winner. This doesn't mean that if you win you'll be asked to say anything nice about the company or its products. You might ask, "Will the company use my name in future advertisements?" One national company answers firmly, "No, not without your permission." Some promoters may have the secret hope that you'll be inclined to say a few nice words, but most, virtually all, won't ask for anything like that.

In the final analysis, the company doesn't really care who gets the prize. All they are interested in is the hoopla that the promotion creates. In the mind of the company, the prize promotion is frequently over long before the closing date. In other words, long before the drawings, long before the prizes are given away, the sweepstakes ad has run its course, and another product has made its debut.

Thus, when Nabisco or other large companies run a sweepstakes, all they care about is will it sell their products? Whether Fred Smith or Jack Jones wins is really of little concern to them.

Chapter Two

MECHANICS OF SWEEPSTAKES

In a sweepstakes, you as a consumer are invited to send in your name, address and proof of purchase, a facsimile of the product, or simply the name of it written on a plain piece of paper. Winners are selected in blindfold drawings.

The interesting thing in sweepstakes is that you have as much chance of winning as anyone else. As a matter of fact, on concluding this book and getting an insight into how winners are selected, you will actually increase your chance of winning. Even if you've never won anything in your life, you'll know all the secrets of how you can win.

The best thing about sweepstakes is that there's absolutely no skill required. Whether you're young or old, bright or dull, you have exactly the same chance of winning. There are countless examples of this fact. You might be an executive in a skyscraper on 42nd Street in Manhattan. You might be a farmer in Idaho. You might be a janitor, a sanitation man, a railway conductor, a housewife. Everybody is eligible to win, and everybody has the same chance.

In one national sweepstakes, Lloyd Milligan, a school principal, entered the name of his school and won $5000 badly needed for repairs. Mrs. James Graham of Litchfield, Connecticut, won a new car. Her husband didn't believe she had won until he saw the car in the driveway. A Missouri minister named Philip B. Settle won a substantial prize and later admitted that he had almost forgotten to send back his entry because he so little expected to win.

A school principal, a housewife, a minister. Who knows? Next time it could be you.

Some sweepstakes theoretically are not open to everybody. In the first place, you are usually not allowed to enter a sweepstakes if you are a relative of someone in the firm or of the judging organization.

But also, certain sweepstakes are geared toward the people who are most likely to use the product that the company is promoting. In direct-mail sweepstakes, major companies only mail out entries to the people who they believe are most likely to purchase their magazines, books, records, or other products. Of course, even if you have no interest in these products, you are entitled to enter if you receive a form in the mail, and you may enter as many times as you receive forms.

Chances are, you probably won't even get the opportunity to enter a sweepstakes if you aren't a likely candidate for the product being promoted. You probably won't even come across the advertisement. The advertisements you do come across, whether in the mail or in the supermarket, are probably aimed at you as one kind of consumer, and will probably appeal to you. That, after all, is what advertising is all about.

Once you've entered a sweepstakes, the mechanics are fairly simple. For you, there's nothing more to be done. You sit back and wait. But what about the judging organization?

You'll notice in the rules that most sweepstakes say "random drawings." The reason why the rules say drawings is this: In a sweepstakes hundreds of thousands of entries are received. It would be impossible to put all the entries into a large drum, and draw from it. Instead the judges hold a series of drawings in which random samples are selected from each mail sack received. Finally, there is a drawing conducted by a blindfolded person who picks the winners out of a large drum.

Most companies employ an independent judging organization to perform this task and to assure absolute objectivity. The role of the independent judging organization varies. Sometimes it helps to create the theme of honesty and adherence to the rules. This firm might select prize-winning numbers by computer or, in the case of a drawing sweepstakes, handle individual selection of winners.

Of course, in sweepstakes, prizes often go unclaimed. You might think that the judges keep these prizes, give them away to friends, or return them to the original company. Not so. Usually what the judging firm will do is hold another drawing and distribute unclaimed prizes to other people who have mailed in their entry forms. This is done for the safety of the judging company as well as for you. It means that no prizes will go unclaimed. It eliminates the frequent worry on the part of consumers that prizes in sweepstakes are not actually given away.

Some companies take extra precautions to make sure that no mistakes are made. One company sends out a congratulation letter to the grand-prize winner, and then spends months double-checking all other winning numbers. Then they send out the other prizes including everything from lowly steak knives to $5000-cash prizes, automobiles, television sets, and cameras. If you are a winner, you will be notified by mail. If you don't receive a letter, and you want to find out who the big winners were in the sweepstakes, you can get a list from the company about five months after the winners have been announced. This way they double-check. And you double-check. It would be a real pity to miss out just from carelessness.

Chapter Three

SECRETS OF WINNING

What separates the wheat from the chaff? The winners from the losers? By now, no doubt, you're burning to win. Well, here's how to do it.

Rule Number 1: Enter often. As incredible as it sounds, most people who have never won a sweepstakes simply haven't entered often enough. The statistical fact of life is that the more you enter, the better chance you have to win. This may seem like simple common sense. Well, it is. That's what it takes most of all to win. The sense that's common to an executive and a janitor, a sanitation man and a PTA president.

It's been my experience that most people will enter once, twice, three times. Yet the real professional sweepstakes entrant will sit and write out hundreds of entries. Naturally, his or her opportunity to win is much greater.

Most sweepstakes, you'll note, carry this statement in the rules, "Enter as often as you like." As we've already determined, you may enter with a proof of purchase or without one. Therefore, it's a simple matter of devoting a few hours to gathering up hundreds of entries.

I've personally talked to many winners of major prizes and one statistically accurate fact keeps recurring. That is, the big winners are people who usually enter many times. You create your own luck by the number of times you enter.

I remember a few years ago speaking on the phone to a young woman who was the winner of a trip to Europe. She was, of course, very excited. During the course of the conversation she told me that she had entered over a thousand times.

Now admittedly, she had a postage cost approaching $100. Yet, the fact of the matter is, she won a prize worth in excess of $2500.

This type of approach requires the consumer to recognize that he is gambling, somewhat like buying Irish Sweepstakes tickets or going to the races, playing cards, or playing the tables in Las Vegas, but if you're in the sweepstakes business to win, the first and most important rule is to enter often.

<u>Rule Number 2:</u> Follow the rules. Again, common sense.

In many of the sweepstakes our firm has handled, fully 25 percent of the entries were disqualified on the basis that entrants failed to follow the rules. It seems ridiculous to have to emphasize this meager point, but I do have to emphasize it, and so I will, over and over again.

It's funny. You insist on rules when you're playing baseball. You wouldn't think of hitting the ball with a rolling pin instead of a baseball bat. You wouldn't dare run around a circle instead of a diamond. You would never count one run as two, or forget to tally the score of the opposition. You even hire an umpire to make sure that everything is judged correctly, that as few as possible technical mistakes are made, that everyone in the game follows the rules.

Of course all this makes sense. You wouldn't have a game called baseball if you didn't have certain baseball rules. It's the rules that actually make the game.

In fact, whenever there's a competitive situation, most groups of people have found the need for rules. We have rules to keep one group of people from taking advantage of another group of people. Our country, so famous for its concept of free enterprise, finally had to establish certain laws, not only to protect the consumer from the business magnates, but the magnates from each other, small business-men from big businessmen, employees from their employers, and so forth. The laws became essential to the continued existence of this country.

We probably all, more or less, understand the careful balance this country tries to maintain between the state's laws and the rights of private corporations and individuals who must abide by them. We know that these laws are basic to the very nature of our country and personal safety. And just as we don't break the rules in baseball, most of us don't break the laws of the country.

But for some incomprehensible reason, whenever we're asked to commit anything to paper, we get confused and start forgetting the rules. Remember back in school when the teacher asked you to write an English theme and gave certain specifications that you were expected to follow? Perhaps she said, "Write on only one side of the paper." Or, "Use ink, not pencil." Or, "Use the special theme paper you can buy in the school bookstore." You may have ignored the rules and then wondered why you failed the theme. You probably didn't think about it from her point of view. You didn't realize that it might be harder to read pencil than pen, or writing on both sides or whatever.

You'd be surprised how often this kind of mistake affects your chances in a sweepstakes or contest. You must remember, the rules are there for a reason. They are there to help the judges do their task more easily. And they are there to make things fair and square among all the entrants. Just as there wouldn't be a game without a baseball, there wouldn't be a contest without rules.

In this chapter we will look at what the rules actually mean.

The rules are so simple in most sweepstakes that the average eight-year-old could follow them without any trouble. Yet, incredibly, many potential winners are disqualified.

Just the other day, the grand-prize winner ($10,000) of the promotion we were handling failed to include the name of the product written on a slip of paper or proof of purchase. This simple omission was the difference between his winning or losing.

Anyone in the sweepstakes business will also tell you about the thousands of entries that are received after the closing date of the promotion, simply a waste of the postage money on the part of the contestants, something they could easily have avoided by following the rules.

Often, rules say print your name and address clearly. Again, every sweepstakes judge can tell you of situations where a name or address was illegible, or, even more tragic, was simply left off of the entry form. There is hardly a sweepstakes that goes by in which some "winner" is chosen only to find his name and address has been left off the entry blank, and there is absolutely no way of telling who the entrant was.

Remember, too, that if the rules say "hand print," then don't type. If the rules say "type or print," either choice is acceptable, but it may be preferable to type, simply because typing is the easiest thing in the world to read. Script is almost never acceptable. Be very cautious on this point, since it's sure to make a difference if your entry is drawn.

Rule Number 3:   Know where to spend your time, money, effort and postage. By this, simply examine the sweepstakes and decide whether this sweepstakes is really for you. Don't enter just to be entering. That doesn't make any sense. Again, use your common sense. I warned you. I'll repeat this basic rule over and over again.

If you have time to enter a sweepstakes 100 times, you're definitely better off entering the sweepstakes that you're really interested in than 25 different sweepstakes that you're marginally interested in.

Why?

The value of prizes in sweepstakes may vary from $5000 to $1,000,000. Assuming the sweepstakes contest receives the same number of entries, it's silly and a waste of time to enter those that only offer a few, small prizes.

Besides, some sweepstakes may offer prizes that may not appeal to you.

We recently conducted a sweepstakes in which the prizes were tracts of land. One of the winners wrote and said he had absolutely no interest in a tract of land. I was somewhat dumbfounded as to why he chose to enter when this, in fact, was the prize.

Of course, just because the prizes are not terribly valuable doesn't mean that you shouldn't enter. Sometimes in local and regional sweepstakes, the prizes may have lesser retail values. But entries are fewer and this increases your chances of winning. It may be worth your while to win a set of encyclopedias, a black-and-white television, or even an electric warming tray. If you can use the prizes, why not enter? You certainly won't be wasting your time.

We conducted a sweepstakes a few years ago for a small manufacturing firm. They only had a limited budget to promote the 1000 prizes available for lucky winners. As astounding as it may seem, we received only 1300 entries. This meant that well over half the entrants received prizes, a good bargain for anybody, worth both the effort and the postage. The moral of this story is that just because the sweepstakes is small and the prizes few, it doesn't mean you shouldn't take the time to send in your name and address. Besides, winning a small prize may give you just the boost you need to go on and win bigger and better prizes.

If you're a smart contestant, you'll spend your

time factoring in the following two situations. First, what is your feeling as to the number of entries that will be received, and you can guess at this by deciding how widely the promotion is advertised. If you see a sweepstakes in every national magazine you pick up, obviously there will be a great number of entries. It's not unusual for upwards of 3 percent of a magazine's circulation to enter. Therefore, if you see a sweepstakes advertised in *TV Guide, McCalls, Ladies Home Journal* and other big-circulation magazines, it's safe to assume there will be hundreds of thousands or millions of entries.

On the other hand, if you see it only on a take-one form in a supermarket, then chances are there will be fewer entries. Second, what is the value of the prizes and do you really want to receive them?

Rule Number 4: A sweepstakes contestant should always remember that all the foibles of human beings unfortunately are present among judging organizations just as much as they are anywhere else. I don't like to admit it. After all, I spend a lot of time in this business, and I want it to work as efficiently, as smoothly, as correctly as possible. But judges are human, and you can take advantage of this fact.

It seems that no matter how well, how carefully we train our people, they are still subject to human error.

How can the contestant use this fact in his favor?

Well, there are a number of ways.

The idea of judging a sweepstakes probably sounds very exciting to you. It probably is exciting the first, second, or maybe even the third time. But after a while, it becomes a dull and repetitive task.

When the judge does a drawing, it's his job to draw from hundreds of thousands of entries. Among those drawn, he will probably have to redraw at least 25 percent, because at least that many people make mistakes on their entry forms. Needless to say, after the first few drawings, the judge will be looking for ways to brighten up his day.

And you can help.

A large and colorful envelope will sometimes work to the advantage of the contestant. Most sweepstakes are drawn from sealed envelopes. If the judge is not blindfolded, he will notice the bright envelope and perhaps choose it. Even if he is blindfolded, the larger surface area of the envelope is likely to attract attention. Remember that the 3"x5" requirement of the entry form usually only applies to the entry itself, not the envelope. As long as you've correctly followed all the rules of the sweepstakes inside, you can do what you want with the outside.

Another thing, sweepstakes winners are usually chosen in multiple drawings. I explained this before. This is because the thousands and thousands of entries in a national sweepstakes will more than fill a drum. This makes a single drawing highly impractical.

Most companies, ours included, train their people to take an equal sampling from all the mailbags. But again, human nature intervenes. Sometimes the judges are lazy. They don't take as many entries as they need from the early mailbags, and they end up taking most of them from the last mailbag received. Therefore, you'd be wise to wait until later in the promotion to enter, and probably if you do so, you'll increase your chances of winning.

You might think of other ways to attract the attention of the judges. These factors, the color and size of the envelope and the timing of your entry, are not supposed to influence the judges, but sometimes they do.

Of course, it's important to note that, in our experience, independent judging organizations have a very high degree of integrity. Although I say that you should try to influence the judges, I don't mean that you should try anything illegal or unfair. Bribery, or suggested bribery, for example, is out of the question. The judges won't stand for it, and it's a sure way to get yourself in trouble.

Rule Number 5: Be on the lookout for sweepstakes. By this I mean your chances of winning are, again, a function of how often you enter. One way to find sweepstakes entry blanks is to join a sweepstakes service. Some of these services are, however, extremely expensive. One of the best ways is to watch for them in your local supermarket. You can ask the check-out clerks or even the manager to help you. Check window displays. Read the newspapers, magazines, and all your so-called junk mail. To you, no mail is junk. Once you get in the sweepstakes mood, you will constantly be looking for new and different sweepstakes. Remember, your chances of finding the really exciting sweepstakes are a function of your keeping a good watch.

Rule Number 6: Set aside a certain amount of time each day or evening for your hobby. Let's face it, any hobby takes time, and most require a certain amount of time-consuming detail work. If you've ever collected stamps, you know that the pleasure of getting unusual or valuable stamps is always followed by the job of hinging the stamps into your album. Or, if you collect tea cups, you have to dust them. If you're a hunter you have to clean your gun and prepare the game for the kitchen.

In the end, all these little tasks seem to add to the pleasure of a job well done. The professional contestant gets to love his pens and pencils, stamps, and stationery, just as much as the stamp collector loves his tongs, stamps, and hinges, and just as much as the fisherman loves his pole. It's all part of the game.

Once you have decided which contests and sweepstakes you wish to enter, you must give yourself enough time to enter correctly. Decide to spend a certain amount of time each day filling out entry forms, addressing envelopes, sponging stamps. Start well in advance of the closing date, and decide exactly how many times you will enter. The number of times you enter should be a sensible figure—not so many times that you'll go stark raving mad filling out forms. And not so few that you don't have a good chance of winning. If you're entering a sweepstakes, you'll send in more entries than if you're entering a contest which requires some skill. And remember, the more difficult the contest, the less steep the competition. This is one factor that really makes contests worth your while.

Enter each sweepstakes one or more times a day during the period when entries are being accepted. You will not be able to enter contests this often, but in the case of sweepstakes, it's not only wise but necessary. In most national sweepstakes there are thousands of entrants, so you must make the law of averages work for you. The more you enter, the more your chances of winning are increased. If you spread out your entries over the duration of the contest, you should increase your chances many times. And, of course, you should send in a batch of entries near the end just on the chance the judges choose most of the entries from the final mailbag.

This is the purpose of setting up a special time each day for your hobby.

Professional contestants who use this technique find that they can win many, many prizes. They win everything from movie cameras to television sets, cash prizes, and cars. You name it, they win it. Some hobbyists win one prize a week. If you intend to be a serious sweepstakes contestant, you must treat the game as seriously as the professionals do. You must enter each sweepstakes often and with deliberation, giving much thought to the kind of sweepstakes, the prizes offered, and your techniques for winning. If you follow these few simple rules, you're bound to win a share of the prizes.

Rule Number 7: Read the rules carefully to make sure the sweepstakes or contest is legal in your state. Some states have stricter laws than others. If the contest is not legal in your state, there's hardly any point in your entering. After all, there are legal sweepstakes in all 50 states, so you should have no trouble finding one to enter.

Also, in some contests or sweepstakes, the rules specifically state that the residents of certain states are not required to send proof of purchase along with their entry blank. If this applies to you in the state where you live, simply send in the alternative 3"x5" card.

Chapter Four

OFFICIAL RULES

To the uninitiated, official rules often appear to be written in legal jargon. But basically, these rules always mean what they say, so it's very important that you understand them.

I want to make sure you're doing everything right, so as a simple exercise, I'm going to lead you through the labyrinth of an official set of rules. When we're finished, you'll be an expert. After all, it would be a pity to spend all that time and money and effort on entering sweepstakes, and then be disqualified just because you're making a few simple mistakes.

Besides, once you understand one set of rules, you'll have no trouble understanding them all. They are all pretty much the same. This doesn't mean that you should ever stop reading them. Occasionally the details do differ. *Always,* but always, read the rules. And with my help, you should have no trouble understanding them and following them correctly.

Rule Number 1: *Print your name, address and zip code on this official entry blank or on a plain piece of paper, 3"x5".*

There is no particular need to use official entry blanks. Obviously if you want to enter a few hundred times you'll have a lot of trouble obtaining that many entry blanks. Your chances of winning are the same whether you enter on an official entry blank or a plain piece of paper.

Plain 3"x5" pads are available in almost any stationery store. This, by the way, is the exact size of an index card. Although index cards tend to be more expensive than plain pads of paper, they are often more readily available. For this reason, the extra expense may be worth it.

Also, the rule says to print your name and address. The reason for this is obvious. The judges have to read thousands of entries, and it's important for you as well as them to make their work as easy as possible.

Writing or script letters will eliminate your chances of winning. Some contests or sweepstakes even forbid typing. The best idea is to print as legibly as possible.

Another thing to watch out for is the zip code requirement.

Leaving out your zip code may make the difference between getting a prize and not getting a prize. Certain prizes are shipped by third-class mail and the post office requires zip codes on all third-class mail.

The manufacturer, the independent judging organization, or whoever chooses the winning entries often will eliminate your entry because you did not follow the rules and include your zip code.

Rule Number 2: *Send the box top from Company X, or the name of the product printed in block letters on a plain piece of paper, 3"x5". You can enter as often as you like, but entries must be mailed separately. All entries must be received no later than November 1, 19——.*

In a sweepstakes, your chances of winning are the same whether you purchase the product or not. This is not necessarily true in the case of contests. In contests, the element of chance is eliminated which means that it is acceptable for the manufacturer to request that you buy his product. But in a sweepstakes, the manufacturer can't ask you to buy anything. Make sure you use a separate 3"x5" piece of paper, if this is what is required.

Again, on a regular basis, we see consumers use the back of the sheet of paper on which they've written their name and address, an old letterhead, old envelopes, or anything but the piece of paper required for the printed name of the product. Believe me, this is not the time and place to save a couple of pennies. Make sure you use a separate piece of paper, and make sure you print.

Samples of block letters are shown below.

VENTURA

VENTURA

VENTURA

In the mind of the judge, block letters mean non-cursive, printed letters. As you can see, there's more than one type of block letter.

The rule, "enter as often as you like," obviously means what it says, but the key is to mail each entry separately. Any independent judging organization can tell you about crateloads of entries which were received with separate entry blanks and special proofs of purchase but were packed together in one box. Obviously, these entries were not acceptable.

As I've said before, entries must be mailed separately. If you are sending in 10 entries, you must send each in a separate envelope. If you are sending in 10,000 entries, you must send in 10,000 separate envelopes, each with an entry form correctly filled out, and, a separate proof of purchase or 3"x5" slip of paper with the name of the product printed on it.

The mail-receipt date is the date by which the entry must be received by the independent judging organization. Unfortunately, the postal service in this country is not known for its efficiency. This is not your fault, but the judging organization doesn't care who the guilty party is. Your entry is either there, or it isn't. If it's not there, you can be sure you won't win any prizes.

Always allow adequate time for your entry to reach the judging organization. It is just dreamy to believe that you can mail an entry a day or two before it is required to be received, even if you live in the same city as the judging organization.

Another word of caution. Neatness and consideration for the judges play a large part in qualifying your entry. Most judges are irritated by what may seem to you the most unlikely things. Avoid stapling your entry form to the proof of purchase. In most cases the judge has to detach them, and he won't do it. He'll probably just throw both away.

One reason why it says in the rules to send in a *separate* piece of paper is that this simple courtesy to the judges makes it easier to read the name and address on your entry form. I recommend you make this task as simple as possible. Also, keep your papers clean. There's nothing less appealing to a tired judge than black ink smears and soiled paper.

Rule Number 3: *All winners will be determined in random drawings conducted by an independent judging organization.*

Firms like ours specialize in the design and implementation of prize promotions. One of the services that we perform is the actual drawing of the entries. The technique which we use for drawing entries has been outlined earlier.

Rule Number 4: *No substitutions are made in the awarding of prizes. Only one prize is allowed per family. Winning odds are determined by the number of entries received. All prizes will be given away.*

These rules mean pretty much what they say. Earlier I talked about entering sweepstakes offering prizes that you don't care about. Winning is not everything. You must remember that even if you win, you can't choose your prize. The prize is chosen for you. You'll know what the prizes are from the original sweepstakes ad.

One reason why you can't expect substitutions is that many companies receive the prizes free from other companies. This may not make much sense to you, but it's a good advertising ploy for a company to give away its products. In other cases, the prizes are purchased by the company in advance. You can be sure if a company has a brand-new Oldsmobile parked in their lot waiting for a lucky winner, they won't trade it in for a Chevy.

"No substitutions" means you get what you win and you win what you get. So if you don't want the Oldsmobile, enter another sweepstakes.

In some cases, only one prize is allowed per family. Many companies feel that it would not look right for the same family to win two or more prizes. To the casual onlooker, it looks like one family is winning everything or as though there is collusion of some sort.

However, one prize per family is not always the rule. In some sweepstakes, one family is allowed more than one prize. This is most often true when the prizes are small.

The matter of odds is simple enough to understand. If 1,000,000 contestants enter the sweepstakes, your chances of winning will be fewer than if 1000 contestants enter. In both cases the sweepstakes might be otherwise exactly the same, but in the latter case, the judge has to select from only a few entries. Naturally, yours is more likely to be chosen.

The rule, "all prizes will be given away," is a very important one. Many people are very suspicious of independent judging organizations. They feel that the judges are awarding prizes only to their friends. And they believe that the prizes are never given away.

Of course, that just isn't true.

State and federal governments place very strict regulations on promotion companies. They pay very close attention to how sweepstakes and contests are handled by these agencies. A firm can make just one slip and that could be the end.

Often companies hold special drawings to determine which entrants will receive the prizes that have gone unclaimed. In other words, even when someone fails to claim his prize, that prize still remains part of the contest and doesn't go back either to the judging firm or the original advertiser.

Rule Number 5: *The winner must take all responsibility for local, state, and federal taxes on his prize.*

This rule does not always hold true. Some sweepstakes offer to pay the taxes, but in this case, the winner must list the additional income on his tax forms.

Usually, however, the winner is responsible for all taxes. In a later chapter I'll explain how to deal with this dreary fact. In the case of lotteries where the winnings are extraordinarily large, payment of the prizes, say of $1,000,000, is made over a period of years so that the tax bite is smaller.

Rule Number 6: *Sweepstakes are open to residents of Hawaii and the continental United States. Contestants must be at least 21 years of age. Employees and the families of employees of the sponsoring company, the independent judging organization, and the advertising company are not eligible. Void where prohibited by law. All federal, state and local laws apply. No purchase or remittance is required.*

The geographical requirements are self-explanatory. If the rule says you must be a resident of the continental United States or Hawaii in order to be eligible, this means that if you live in Puerto Rico, you are not eligible. If you live in Spain, you are not eligible. If you live anywhere outside the United States, you are not eligible.

Entrants need not always be 21 years of age, so read the rules carefully. But if you are required to be 21 years old, and you are not, and you win, sure enough the judging organization will discover this. If you win a big prize you will be investigated by a detective agency to substantiate the fact that you were eligible to enter and that you complied with all the rules. So don't try to pull the wool over anybody's eyes. If you really want to enter, you can always have an adult enter for you.

Employees of the sponsoring company, the advertising company, and the independent judging organization are not eligible to enter for obvious reasons. Suppose one of these people entered and won. Even though the contest is judged fairly, the general public is bound to have its doubts. It just doesn't look very good. So if you have a relative involved with a sweepstakes, keep out of that one. It would just be a waste of your time.

"Void where prohibited by law" means that even a national contest is subject to state and local laws and regulations. Some sweepstakes are legal in all the 50 states. Others are not. Read the rules carefully, and check into your own state laws. To find out about individual state laws, write Office of the Attorney General at the State Capitol in your own state. Ask for a copy of laws governing sweepstakes, lotteries and/or prize promotions. It would be a shame to spend your time and money on a contest for which you weren't eligible.

In a sweepstakes, no remittance and no purchase is necessary because this fact is precisely what makes a sweepstakes legal. As you'll remember, lotteries are only legal when run by state or federal governments. Private companies are not allowed to run lotteries, but they are allowed to run certain kinds of prize promotions. What makes a sweepstakes different from a lottery is the fact that no consideration is present. In other words, instead of having to buy a chance or a ticket, you are allowed to enter for free.

What about all these rules? Well, it's extremely important that you follow all of them carefully. They are so simple! If you make a mistake, your entry, even if it's a winner, will be disqualified. Therefore, I suggest that you take special care with the first entry and copy this one as many times as you enter that contest. When you're reading the rules, underline the important points that you'll need to remember. Use a pen with bright ink, and make sure that you underline the closing date. But remember, each rule is important, and in order to win, you must follow all the rules.

Are you ready to begin?

Good luck!

I'm sure there's a prize waiting for you.

Chapter Five

PROFESSIONAL TIPS

Here are some often overlooked tips that can help you win more sweepstakes.

Tip Number 1: Separate the tasks of entering sweepstakes.

Henry Ford taught us a long time ago that assembly-line operations get more work done faster.

If you divide up the tasks of entering the sweepstakes, you'll find that you get more done in less time. For instance, first put all the stamps on the envelopes, then fill out all the qualifiers. You might even be able to get the rest of the family involved in this. Set up an assembly-line production. Have one person sponge on the stamps. Have another person print out the block-letter proofs of purchase. Have another person fill out entry forms. Have another person fill envelopes and seal them.

Remember, the key to winning is entering often.

And this way you can enter twice as often in the same amount of time.

Tip Number 2: Abbreviate as much as possible. Find a way to abbreviate your name and address. Again, in this way you'll find that you can enter more often. Obviously, "NE" for Nebraska is going to take a lot less time than spelling out the word, "Nebraska." But here, a word of caution: make sure that it's a common abbreviation, one that's known to the judging organization. If the judge can't understand what you've written, he'll disqualify your entry. Don't ever invent abbreviations. If you have a question, look up words in the dictionary. It will take more time the first time, and less time later on.

Tip Number 3: Try to limit your entries to national contests.

As I've said earlier, it's sometimes worthwhile to enter small local contests. Often the number of entries is small in relation to the number of prizes. But if you do enter, make sure you're dealing with a company or organization that you know and trust.

One of the reasons why it's better to enter national contests is that they are usually judged by independent judging organizations. Thus, you are assured of a great deal of fairness and integrity on the parts of the judges.

People often ask me why I have this great trust for independent judging organizations. As I've said before, the judges are simply human beings like you or me. They are not above reproach. They don't really have any special qualifications. But by and large, as a group, I think you'll find them exceedingly honest from the point of personal morality. Also, they are closely governed by any number of federal, state, and local regulatory agencies, including the Federal Trade Commission and the Post Office Department. These judging organizations are watched extremely closely. Of course, if their integrity is ever in question, they're soon out of business.

For these reasons, I think you can enter with a fair amount of confidence if you see that there's an independent judging organization involved. Independent judging organizations are always involved in national contests.

Tip Number 4: Sometimes you'll notice that there are different box numbers in different newspapers, magazines, or on different entry blanks. These are key numbers so that the manufacturer understands where most of the entries are coming from. I suggest that you mail entries to each of these different box numbers. Again, this provides an even distribution of your entries and helps assure you of a maximum chance of winning.

Tip Number 5: Read the rules to make sure the promotion is legal in your state. I can't emphasize this point too much or repeat it too often. Various states at various times have some legislation restricting sweepstakes. If on close reading of the rules, you are to find that in the state of Florida, for example, the sweepstakes is void, and you are a resident of that state, it would be silly to waste your time and postage to enter that sweepstakes, for even if your entry was drawn it would immediately be disqualified.

One reason for the voiding of certain states at times is that the company does not market its products there.

But most often, say around 90 percent of the time, voiding occurs simply because the particular kind of prize promotion that company is offering isn't allowed in the state.

If this is true for you, in your state, and you wish to enter a sweepstakes that's prohibited by law, don't write the advertiser. You can be sure that he cares as much about this as you do. Instead, write to your state legislators and suggest that they have a hard look at the sweepstakes laws because they are unfair to you as a resident of that state.

Chapter Six

CONTESTS

According to legend, Christopher Columbus, himself, was supposed to be the first sponsor in the New World. He offered a prize to the sailor who first spotted land. The story has it that when he was actually informed of the hazy presence of land in the distance, he kept the prize to himself.

Contests, as I indicated earlier, require a certain amount of skill. They come in a variety of forms such as "complete this statement in 25 words or less," jingles, and rhymes.

What distinguishes a contest from a sweepstakes is the element of skill. Contests were especially popular in the forties and fifties and today contests are enjoying a comeback.

There are several reasons why manufacturers prefer sweepstakes over contests. First of all, contests do not draw great numbers of entries. Most people feel that it takes too much time and effort to enter a contest that requires skill and they are less likely to do so. Remember, the manufacturer is interested in getting a lot of exposure.

Second, contests have post-promotion problems. That is, you write 25 words and somebody else writes 25 words and usually there is a degree of subjective judgment as to which one is better. Remember, the sponsor is interested in having you like him, and he is not looking for post-promotion letters in which you write and say that your entry was better than that which won a prize.

In addition, this problem has been the grounds for numerous legal suits in which independent judging organizations were required to prove in court that the entry selected was, in fact, superior. Of course, this problem is not present in sweepstakes where somebody dashes off an entry in a minute.

If all this is true, why are there contests at all?

First, as you may well imagine, sponsors and advertising companies can often obtain ideas from the consumer that will help them promote a certain product. In some contests, there's a veritable gold mine of appealing ideas and entries. In a sweepstakes, the sponsor gets nothing but a name and address on a bit of paper. But in a contest he actually may get an endorsement, a rhyme, or a jingle of some advertising value.

Second, for a long time sweepstakes, unlike contests, were under a lot of harsh federal, state and local legislation. Hence the growth of contests. Fortunately, most of these laws have been abolished.

Since a contest differs from a lottery you may, under the law, be required to buy the product and send in an actual proof of purchase. If this is the case and you don't comply with the requirement, your entry will be void.

But it should be noted that the actual purchase of the product is probably as much to your advantage as it is to the sponsor's. After all, if you are going to write something about this product, you ought to be familiar with it. One of the important qualities the judges look for in your entry is sincerity. Naturally, if you're familiar with the product, you'll be better able to judge and amplify its special virtues. You'll be familiar with all its best selling points. In short, you'll know what to say.

The rules of a contest must clearly state on what .basis the contest will be judged. The rules may say something like creativity, 30 percent; originality, 40 percent; aptness of thought, 30 percent; or some variation of this.

Originality usually means the ability to take commonplace, everyday ideas and express them in a different or uncommon way.

It's best to explain what originality means to a judging organization by the U.S. Patent Office requirement by which new patents are given. The patent office says, "The invention or discovery of any new and useful art, machine, manufacturer . . . or any new and useful improvements thereof."

This means that the contestant must sit down and think about the problem from a different light. If the question is, "complete in 25 words or less, 'I like Sweet Love soap because . . . ,'" to say, "because it gets me clean," is hardly an original thought. However, it requires very little intelligence to come up with an original thought in this case. All that's required is to sit and think about the cleanliness process, or what Sweet Love soap does in a number of different ways. You might not only think of the process of cleanliness, but also you might consider sweetness of smell or softness of skin.

Of course the words "Sweet Love" suggest other important qualities. Women might be concerned with the problem of how to get clean without washing the oils out of their skin. Men might worry about the long-lasting effects of a soap, how to get clean, smell nice, and stay sweet-smelling for a long period of time. Of course, the very good side effect of being clean and smelling sweet is that these things make you good company for your sweetheart.

All of these ideas can be clearly and cleverly stated in a number of different ways.

Many people wonder why they never see winning entries published. Sponsors never send out copies of the winning entries. The reason behind this is to prevent the great disappointment among those who entered and didn't win. In the early fifties, when the practice was to distribute winning entries, the result for the sponsor was disastrous. Many people had labored long and hard on their entries and were totally convinced that their work was better than the winner's. They were left with feelings of ill-will toward the sponsor and at times even instituted legal action. It is important to remember that advertisers view prize offers as a promotion technique. Therefore, they have found it counterproductive to offer copies of winning entries that might result in negative feelings for the losers.

Contests also frequently require aptness. Aptness simply means whether or not the entry relates to the subject of the contest. All too many completions of the statement, "I like Sweet Love soap because. . . ." have had little to do with soap. In other words, you wouldn't dream of recommending the soap for a shoe polish or an effective barrier against your mother-in-law. Save all these other clever thoughts for another contest. Inappropriateness of thought is all too common in contest entries.

Here it is important to note that while judges appreciate originality and aptness, it's wise to avoid an excess of cleverness. In other words, a message that's clear and easily understood is far superior to one that's difficult to figure out because of excessive ingenuity. When entering contests, remember this one basic rule: Make sure the judges get the whole message at a single, quick reading. This rule applies for two reasons. First, your entry should be as easy to understand as an advertisement. Have you ever seen an advertisement that you couldn't understand in a matter of seconds? Secondly, the judges are reading thousands of entries, and by the time they get to yours, they may simply be too exhausted to comprehend the finer points.

The third important ingredient of a good contest entry is sincerity. Sincerity is a double-edged sword in the contest-judging business.

On the one hand, a manufacturer running a contest such as, "I like Sweet Love soap because . . . ," is not truly interested in honesty. To a great degree, he is interested in flattery and hearing good things about his product.

How is one sincere and flattering, but not to the point of dishonesty? This very point may make the difference between a truly good contest entry and a mediocre one. And, the answer is not apparent to most people.

The question, "How does one become sincere?" is a question that people ask all the time about relationships, about business, about life. It's a difficult question to answer—both relative to life, and relative to a contest.

Sincerity is probably easier to attain in a contest than in life, for sincerity in a contest is simply the outward appearance of honesty. Your total relationship to the judging organization is based on this single letter. All that is necessary is to project the feeling of sincerity in your letter.

A warning. When you first get the idea to enter, you might sit down and dash off a series of entries on sheer inspiration. But remember, even the greatest of poets never tries to publish the 15 minutes following his creation. He gives himself time to disagree with himself. He gives himself time to hone and improve his work, to embellish it or tone it down. It's very important for him to create the appropriate tone, the exact syntax that will convey his meaning.

When you enter a contest, consider yourself a professional writer.

You should give yourself what many contest experts call a cooling period. This means after the first rush of inspiration, the first torrent of words, you set aside your creative efforts for at least six or seven days. Look again. Reevaluate your little poem, your jingle, your sentence completion..

At this point, you will be more objective. You'll be able to spot incorrectness of tone, insincerity, ineptness, or any other flaw that might make your brainchild a losing entry. Don't be afraid to improve your original thought. Make verbs and adjectives stronger. Delete useless and ineffectual words. Be supercritical. At this point, you are your own best judge, so don't be too nice.

If you're an experienced contestant, you'll probably want and need other friends in the same business. Probably the best source of information is Eggleston Enterprises, Milford, New York 13807. Send a self-addressed stamped envelope to them for details. Try to correspond frequently with others who have the same hobby. Tell them what you have done recently. Discuss your entries with them. Find out what they have done, and discuss their winning entries. Sometimes it's inspiring to know about the work of others.

Poets and other writers do this often. They have workshops and readings where they share each other's work. It's a good idea for contest hobbyists to do this, too. It keeps your mind from getting stale, and helps ensure fresh and exciting new ideas for future entries.

But another word of warning. It's never a good idea to actually copy someone else's work. You may think this point is obvious, yet many contestants have done this in the past, and some have even won cash prizes for doing so. No judge can be familiar with every winning entry in every contest published throughout the country. So, in fact you have a chance of slipping through a plagiarized prize winner.

But I don't recommend that you do this. First of all, you can't be sure that the judge won't recognize your entry. And second, from the standpoint of enjoying your hobby, how can you, if you don't play fair? After all, if you're playing baseball, you don't expect the umpire to suspend the rules so you can make a home run on a single base hit. The game wouldn't be any fun if you didn't follow the rules strictly. And entering contests won't be any 'un for you if you win unfairly.

When you actually sit down to write, you should keep something else in mind. Naturally the sponsors and judges will be inclined in your favor if you convey to them the idea that you have used and will use their product in the future. After all, the contest is a promotion for their product, and if you are a happy user of that product, they will more likely be happy donors of a gift. Keep in mind that you are a potential consumer to the sponsor. This fact is as important to him as the sincerity and aptness of your entry.

At this point it might be worthwhile to add that one of the characteristics frequently not stated in the rules as a requirement of winning is neatness. However, I can tell you that this could be one of the crucial parts of your entry's success.

Unfortunately, or fortunately, as the case may be, only human beings are reading the entries. Perhaps at some future date independent judging organizations will employ computers to do the reading for them. But at present, the organizations can only employ human beings.

Picture a room with 250,000 to 400,000 entries. Your task from nine in the morning until five at night is to read through those entries. Your eyes become bleary and you become tired. And, no matter how diligent you are, how interested in the job, if a letter is smudged and dirty, pencil-written or creased, it can contain the most brilliant thoughts in the world, but it's hard to become enthused about it.

Any high school teacher can tell you that a neat presentation is often a large part of the battle in winning a good grade. If you enter a contest, remember this and if you learn nothing else from this book, you've already gotten your money's worth.

Neatness is obviously one of the most important qualities, but this doesn't mean that you need to type an entry. In fact, handwritten entries, neat and legible, frequently have a greater appeal than type-written entries in the minds of the judges.

Again, we are talking about judges in a rather nebulous way, for judges have any number of different characteristics since they are individuals. Understanding and coming to grips with this fact, and knowing that your opportunity to win is based on impressing people, will surely increase your chances of winning.

One way to preserve the neatness of your entry is to mail it flat and backed by a heavy piece of cardboard. This mailing technique prevents the entry from becoming creased and thus illegible. It may cost a little more to mail your entry this way, but if you believe your entry is really good, you can improve your chances of winning by presenting it in this fashion. So often entries are received creased and smudged, illegible, and dirty. You can be certain that any judge is very grateful to receive one that is neat and clean.

Another similar technique is to use the same 3"x5" cards you have been using for sweepstakes. The slightly heavy cardboard will not be so easily damaged in the mail or by hasty clerks slicing open envelopes by machine.

Some contestants decorate their entries with fancy

drawings. These pictures are either drawn or clever cutouts from magazines. The idea is to attract the judge's attention, and, as I have already said, the judges are only human. Although, in local contests added decorations may make some difference, in a national contest, the judges find these fancy decorations an annoyance. In the interest of fairness, most judges really do not want to be influenced by such externals.

I offer you a simple rule. In national contests, avoid the use of extra decorations, fancy pictures, flowers, fruits, clouds, whatever. In local contests, use all your ingenuity to attract the attention of the judges.

The envelope, however, is fair game. Use large, bright-colored envelopes, and if you have an instinct to decorate, use it here. Decorative envelopes have no bearing on the actual entries. The entry inside is safe, plain, and easy to read. But a bright and fancy envelope may very well attract the attention of the judge. It may please him at a moment when he's feeling most unpleased, tired, hot, cranky after a long day.

One of the most important factors for you to keep in mind is the closing date. In this way, contests are no different than sweepstakes. It's a wise idea to write the date in black ink on your calendar, and if your calendar reveals only one day at a time, write in the date each day for a full week before the contest closes. This will help you avoid the mistake of sending in your entries too late.

If you haven't got a calendar, consider it just another necessary expense of your hobby. All things considered, it's a relatively inexpensive hobby, but you do need a few items to keep yourself in business, and one of these is surely a calendar. Another thing—make certain you have a good dictionary. This item probably isn't necessary for your sweepstakes entries, but for contests which depend on skill and intelligence, a dictionary is another necessity. Nothing turns a judge off faster than misspelled words.

If you intend to become a really professional contestant, you might even consider setting aside a certain area in the house for your desk and materials, or a certain amount of office space. This way you can keep everything together, including paper, index cards, pens, stamps, envelopes, a good calendar and a good dictionary.

If you have a special place to do your work, this of course will make it easier for you. You don't have to spend the time each day getting all your materials together. Also, you'll have some place to keep duplicates of all your entries. This is another good idea. First, because you should never send anything without keeping a copy on hand, and second, because when you're having trouble thinking of new ideas, you can look over the old ones and get the creative juices flowing again. You can be sure a writer or poet rereads much of his work. This gives him an idea of his progress, and helps him create new ideas and projects.

Many novice contestants send biographical letters to the sponsors along with their contest entries. They tell long tales of woe, hardship, and misfortune. This is a rather unpleasant form of bribery that seldom, if ever, increases the chances of winning. In fact, such letters are usually thrown away immediately. You'll be very lucky if your entry doesn't end up in the trash can as well if you choose to accompany it with a tale of woe.

After all, a contest is a game and it should be played like a game. You wouldn't expect to win a home run in baseball just because you had a broken leg. You get a home run only by hitting the ball well. It's the same in contests. You can only expect to win if your entries are good, so you shouldn't waste your time writing sad letters. Spend every spare minute writing entries. You can send in as many as you wish, and they will all be considered if they reach the judging organization in time.

Humor, too, should be regarded with a certain amount of respect. If you are bent on being funny, make sure it's appropriate. In most of the short-statement contests, it's better to extol the product and write about its virtues. Humor has little place in such a contest where the main intent is to tell why the product means something to you. In this case, humor might mistakenly poke fun at the product. This approach is sure to alienate the sponsor who wants to hear only good things.

In more elaborate contests that require essays or clever jingles, humor with taste is more than acceptable. In the case of jingles, it's often wise to limit humor to the last line. After all, this is how a joke works, isn't it? Everything builds to the punch line. Essays can, of course, benefit from humor throughout.

The tone of your entry is as important as the content. The tone tells the judges who you are, and the good contestant always makes his presence known. Do not hide. Be yourself. Don't use high-falutin language that you wouldn't dream of using in everyday speech. It's usually wise to avoid slang, as well, but the important thing beyond this is to speak plainly from your heart. You, the individual, are the person who's going to make this entry different and special. You're the one who's going to make it a winner. You can be sure you won't do this by pretending you're somebody else.

And while I'm on the subject, many contestants believe they should use somebody else's name. Remember, you're allowed to win as many prizes as you actually win. Just because you've won a few contests, doesn't mean it's illegal or unacceptable for you to win again. That's the whole point, after all, of becoming a professional contestant. Actually, using an assumed name may cause you more harm than good. If you win a large prize, you're certain to be investigated, and when this investigation takes place your real name will be discovered. In this case, judges may become suspicious. They may choose to abandon your entry for another one that seems more on the up and up.

About Winning

"Congratulations, you're a winner. . . ." This is the letter that is music to a contestant's ear.

All that's really necessary, at this point, is to sit back and wait for your prize. But all too often, contestants become flustered.

First of all, if the prize is valuable enough, you will be investigated by an independent detective agency. Also you will probably be required to sign an affidavit.

It is important for you to understand that the

purpose of the investigation is to protect the sponsor who wants to make sure, in fact, that you complied with all the rules. By chance, for example, if you were to enter the Minute Miss Sweepstakes and your brother worked for Minute Miss company, you would not be eligible. Suppose this fact later leaked out. Even if your brother had nothing to do with the fact that you won, the sponsor's potential embarrassment would be great.

- This is the important reason why contests and sweepstakes say in the rules that you cannot enter if you are related to a member of the sponsor's firm, the advertising firm, or the independent judging organization.

Also, remember that a prize cannot be taken away from you just because you do not impress the investigatory agency. The purpose of the investigation is simply to make sure that you followed all the rules and won the contest fair and square. So don't get nervous. Don't refuse to see the detective, and answer his questions honestly, not evasively. The detective agency has nothing to do with the actual contest, and is in no position to judge you or your winning entry. This is not their job. You and your entry have already been judged and selected.

The detective agency will provide you, most likely, with a statement to sign. The statement is very honest, open, and aboveboard. It simply says that you have complied with the rules.

I have heard many horror stories about prizes being taken away from contestants because they made a poor impression. People often think that contestants are sometimes demoted to lower prizes.

I can tell you that these stories are absolutely untrue!

The detective agencies that sponsors use to check out contestants, such as Pinkerton and Burns, have no authority over the sweepstakes. I repeat, their job is simply to make sure that you have followed the rules.

Chapter Seven

QUESTIONS AND ANSWERS

This chapter will answer the common questions asked about contests and sweepstakes.

Q: I understand that professional judging organizations keep a list of people who have won too often. Is this true?

A: Absolutely untrue. Winners are selected in exact accordance with the rules. Whether you've won one contest or a hundred is of little interest to the independent judging organization.

Sometimes rules will state, "one prize to a family." This pertains to that particular contest, so even though you actually were drawn three times, you would receive the first or major prize that was drawn.

This is another reason why it makes no sense to enter under an assumed name. Since judging organizations do not keep lists, and since the sponsor cares little about who wins the prize, you might as well use your own name. This will serve to make the investigation easier when and if you actually do win something big.

Q: Are sweepstakes ever fixed? "I feel this because I see a lot of the same names on winners' lists."

A: In our experience, there has never been a national or regional sweepstakes involving a major advertiser that has been fixed in any way. The judging organization and the company just wouldn't take the risk that is involved.

The last national contest I heard of that was fixed happened many years ago in France. That was in the time of Louis the XIV. In this case, he and several of his top courtiers won top prizes in a drawing. The king was finally so embarrassed by this event, that he ordered all the prizes returned and redistributed.

Of course, I can't vouch for local storekeepers who run local contests.

The integrity of a local contest depends solely on the integrity of the store or company that runs such a contest. If you have any questions at all, my advice is to avoid such contests.

In other words, if a local stationery store runs a sweepstakes and the owner does the drawing or sees to the drawing himself, there is hardly any regulatory agency that will oversee this. Of course, most local stores depend on the goodwill of the surrounding community, so I don't mean to impugn anyone's integrity. By and large, you can expect to have your entry judged fairly, even in local contests.

You may still be wondering why you see the same

names on a number of winners' lists. This relates directly to the fact that the more times you enter, the more likely you are to win. Many contestants who enter frequently find that they are frequent winners. A lot of names that come up over and over are the names of people who have spent many hours entering sweepstakes.

Q: How can I find out about sweepstakes and contests?

A: There are any number of clipping services around the country which an avid contestant can subscribe to. These become extremely expensive because many of them charge up to $100 a month. Other sources are contest clubs which provide this information. A third source is simply a good check of your supermarket and you should ask your supermarket manager or storekeeper to save entry blanks for you. A fourth source is various newsletters that are available on the subject.

Q: When entering a contest that says, "Complete this statement in 25 words or less . . . ," and the statement starts, "I like Sweet Love Soap because . . . ," do the 5 words "I like Sweet Love Soap because" count toward the 25 words in my answer?

A: No. The statement says, "*Complete* this sentence in 25 words or less." It is like saying, add 25 words or less to the introductory statements.

Q: Why can't I receive a cash substitute for a prize that I have won that I'm not particularly interested in?

A: Sometimes companies receive the prizes that

they are giving away free in exchange for the advertising value. So, for example, if the first prize is a car being given away in the XYZ Company Sweepstakes, XYZ may have, in fact, paid very little for the car or received it free in exchange for the national advertising that it received. Therefore, the sponsors of the contest actually have taken ownership of the car and must award it.

However, you can always sell a prize which you have received in a sweepstakes. Therefore, you can turn almost any prize of value into some sort of cash award.

Q: Why do sponsors prefer printing to writing on contest entry forms?

A: I have probably already answered this question many times over. The answer is obvious. Contest judges have found that the majority of hand-writing on entries is poor. Therefore they ask for printing which is almost always easier to read.

Q: What is the difference between these words in the rules: "a sheet of paper," "a piece of paper," "a card"?

A: When the rules say you should use a sheet of paper, this means use a piece of standard size paper without lines. A standard-size sheet of paper measures $8\frac{1}{2}$ by 11 inches and folds for a standard-size envelope. This means that a legal sheet or a piece of paper torn from a legal pad is not acceptable.

A piece of paper can mean almost any size unless a certain size is specified. The usual size specified is 3"x5" and you can substitute a standard index card, if you wish. However, if the rules specify a 3"x5" card, don't substitute a piece of paper. Cards are sturdier, don't crease as easily, and often pass through the mail with less wear-and-tear. This means the judges can read entries from cards with more facility.

Q: What does the sponsor mean when he says he wants you to print your entry on a plain, 3"x5" sheet of paper?

A: He means that in this case, 3"x5" is the only size acceptable and the paper or card should be unruled.

Q: What kinds of contests are there?

A: Probably as many kinds of contests as you could possibly imagine, and some that you couldn't.

There are completion contests which require you to complete sentences. There are limerick contests which usually give part of the final limerick in the rules and require you to complete it. For instance, a limerick might begin like this:

> There was an old man from Rome,
> Who had his old head in a tome,
> And when past turned to present,
> He found it more pleasant. . . .

You have to finish it in the appropriate number of words.

There are fiction contests which require the contestant to submit stories, even novels. Often large prizes are awarded the winners of such contests, and publication of the first- and sometimes second-prize pieces.

There are contests which require contestants to

name dogs or horses, and the most original and appropriate names win.

There are children's contests in which only kids are allowed to enter. These, however, are usually a farce. It would be impossible to prevent the child's relatives, friends and teachers from helping to compose the entry.

There are contests which comprise the correct solutions to puzzles, acrostics, crossword puzzles and the like.

There are recipe contests in which the entrant is supposed to invent his own recipe using some product or another.

You have only to leaf through a newspaper and magazine to find any number of scintillating tests and contests. You can be sure that there's scarcely an idea that hasn't already been thought of.

Q: Why should I spend most of my time and effort on entering national contests?

A: I have given you the answer to this question many times over. You know, for one, that national contests are never fixed and that they are judged independently. This means, I repeat, that your entry will be judged fairly. National contests are well regulated by government agencies. This is for your protection.

Also, national contests often offer more prizes, the largest prizes, and cash prizes. This makes them more worthwhile.

Q: If I win a prize must I pay income tax on it?

A: Absolutely yes. How you go about this will be explained later. There is much confusion about whether a winner has to pay taxes on the full price of a car or an item of furniture. I will talk about this in Chapter Eight on taxes.

Q: Should I spend time on only one type of contest?

A: No. Especially if you are a novice. In the first place, you must find out what types of contests you are suited to. You may think you are good at one kind. The judges may think you're good at another. Besides, the contests that are easiest to win usually have the greatest odds. In the beginning it's best to try your hand at many different kinds of sweepstakes and contests. Later, after some experience, you can narrow down the field.

Q: When a contest or sweepstakes gives me the option of sending a boxtop, qualifier, or a 3"x5" card, which of these is best?

A: All give you equal chances of winning as long as you're a good block-printer. In a sweepstakes, the sponsor is not legally permitted to request a boxtop or any other proof of purchase. The judges must treat each entry equally. But if you are unsure of your printing, it might be more effective for you to send a boxtop or qualifier. Of course, if you are sending hundreds of entries, this will probably be impossible.

Q: What is the difference between the "sponsor," the "independent judging agency," "the advertising company," and the "detective agency"?

A: You may not believe it, but all these firms are different. First of all, at the top of the hierarchy is the sponsor. The sponsor is the company that owns the original product. This product is the reason for the sweepstakes or contest. The sweepstakes is created to promote this product—that is, introduce it to the buying public, or help it to sell better.

The sponsor usually hires a promotion company or an advertising company to give advice in the promotion of the product and to devise the sweepstakes or contest more appropriate to the product and to the manufacturing company.

The promotion company or the sponsor hires an independent judging organization to handle the mechanics of the contest, the drawings, the awarding of prizes. This prevents anyone from thinking, however unjustifiedly, that the winners are somehow "inside."

The detective agency, usually hired by the sponsor, is again an independent agency. The purpose of the detective agency is to investigate big winners and make sure they complied with all the rules.

Q: What do you mean when you talk about a professional contestant?

A: Well, really nothing mysterious. What I call a professional contestant is the person who enters many contests, and because he enters often and enters correctly, he wins more often. Hardly a day goes by that he doesn't anticipate the postman's foot on his front porch. Hardly a week goes by that he doesn't win a prize.

The professional contestant may or may not belong to a clipping service or club. He probably doesn't need a clipping service by the time he becomes truly professional. He's probably too busy entering to worry about what he's going to enter next. Besides, his is a trained eye. He rarely misses an ad in the supermarket or in the newspaper.

A club has more advantages. In a club he can meet and become friendly with other professional contestants just like himself. Contestants may be able to trade off ideas and to help each other with difficult entries.

But it is not necessary to belong to a club in order to win. Some professional contestants don't have time for such additional activities. They are too busy filling out entry blanks.

Q: Is it possible to get inside information or tips on contests or sweepstakes?

A: I can't swear it's impossible, but I've never known of such a case. Sweepstakes and contests are legal activities and are carefully regulated. If a sponsor's integrity or a judging organization's integrity is ever questioned, both may find themselves out of business. In most cases, it's just too risky to try anything remotely illegal or unfair. And also, most big companies have a great deal of pride in the reputation of their organizations.

Q: I have heard of contests that request the original entry forms or facsimiles. What does this mean?

A: A facsimile is little more than the usually acceptable block-letter substitute. A facsimile should be as close to the original entry blank as possible— this means as to color, size and shape of letters, wordings, all the way down to the last detail.

Q: What is a score sheet?
A: Most judging agencies have score sheets to

help them judge the entries. This enables them to judge each entry on the same points. For example, one outfit has designed a score sheet which offers point totals for various qualities outlined in the rules. That is, the judge scores aptness, originality, creativity, neatness and other qualities and then adds up the score.

Q: Why are there so many rules in even the simplest contests and sweepstakes?

A: Rules, in general, are there to make the contest fair for everyone. They make the contest easy for the judges, easy for the sponsor, easy for the contestants. They offer certain fair limits in which the competition can take place. They make sure that no one gets a better deal than anyone else.

Q: If I win, when and how will I find out about it?

A: This varies from company to company, from contest to contest. Often, many companies notify the grand-prize winners right away. Lesser winners may have to wait several months while the judging organization double-checks winning entries to make sure they are not making any mistakes.

Also, as mentioned earlier, before you receive your prize, you can expect to be investigated to make sure you have followed the rules. This, of course, takes time. Most companies try to take care of these details as fast as possible. They know you are excited, and of course they are happy to give you your prize.

You may be notified by phone or by mail. Form letters are very much alike. Usually, only the size and nature of the prize differs from letter to letter.

Q: Is there any particular type of contest I should avoid?

A: Absolutely yes. Never enter a contest when the name of the sponsor is not clearly visible in the ad. Many contests say something vague like "contest manager." If this is the case, it usually means that something underhanded is going on. You may find that you are supposed to sell books or encyclopedias because you have supposedly "won" this contest. Usually, such a contest is a ploy to make you spend time or money in another way.

Q: What's the most important fact to remember in a completion contest, or a jingle contest?

A: Never copy, and never let anyone else copy you. If your entry is duplicated, both yours and the duplication are likely to be rejected.

Q: Do states vary in their laws and attitudes with regard to contests and sweepstakes?

A: Yes. Some states prohibit sweepstakes or contests. This is of course the reason for the common phrase, "void where prohibited by law." Other states permit sweepstakes, but may, for instance, definitely not require you to show proof of purchase if you enter. Missouri is such a state.

Q: What if I'm just not a lucky person?

A: I'm telling you, there's no such thing. You create your own luck. The more times that you enter, the more likely you are to win. If you make contests your hobby, you will almost certainly win.

Q: If I win, do I need to thank the sponsor for my prize?

A: You don't have to. You might be inclined to. It might be fun to sit down and write a thank-you note. After all, when someone gives you a gift, you perform this simple kindness. It makes the giver feel good. And it probably makes you feel good.

Chapter Eight

WHAT TO DO ABOUT TAXES

At least two things in life are inevitable: death and taxes.

Once a year the forms come in the mail and once a year you must sit down with all your records and figure out if you owe the government, or if the government owes you. One of the commonest complaints of big winners is that they have to pay such high taxes on their prizes. Sometimes, if the prize is large enough, the taxes are as great as 70 percent.

Of course, at this point you're probably wondering how to avoid paying such a high price.

I can tell you from my long experience in this business, that you'd better not try. The government keeps such a close watch over lotteries, sweepstakes, and contests, that you can be sure you'll get caught if you don't pay. In this case you'll find that you owe an additional fine.

It's best to keep everything on the up and up from the very start.

Besides, after all it's only fair. You can't be losing money, since you didn't have the money to begin with.

But how can you get away with paying the least taxes?

I recommend that you consult a tax lawyer, or an agent from your local Internal Revenue Office.

Usually it's done this way.

If the prize is a cash prize, of course, you must declare the entire sum of money and deduct expenses incurred in winning.

If the prize is merchandise, you declare the fair market value of the prize and, again, deduct the expenses incurred in winning.

One little warning: You are never allowed to declare any losses. What does this mean? If you win a couch you're ahead of the game no matter what. If the retail value is $1000, and you sell it for $50, you can't declare the so-called loss of $950. This all has to do with the fair market value, so pay close attention to what follows.

What is the fair market value? The definition of the fair market value is the amount a willing seller, not forced to sell, will demand, and a willing buyer, not forced to buy, will pay.

In other words, let's say you win a car worth $4000. You cannot sell the car to your brother for $50 and declare this amount as the value of the prize on your tax forms. Many people are confused about this very point. Chances are, you could sell the car for an amount pretty close to its so-called retail value, so you'll probably end up having to declare something close to the retail value on your tax forms.

Suppose you win a custom-made couch, made to order for your living room and it comes in bright red only, because you listed your living room colors on your entry form. In this case, the value of the couch has a great deal to do with its measurements and color, and since it was made to order, it probably has a greater value to you than to any prospective buyer. But suppose you decide that you don't want the couch after you win it, and you want to sell it. Selling the couch depends on your finding a willing buyer whose living room is close to the same size as yours, and whose color scheme is the same. It's something like trying to sell a piece of used furniture, and there's nothing you can do about the size and color.

Now, suppose there's only one prospective buyer in your community. If this is the case, you can't honestly insist that your $1000 couch is in great demand. You will probably have to sell it for pretty much what this one buyer is willing to pay. You may try to bargain with him, but he might just walk out the door. You're stuck with a big, red couch that you don't want.

In such a case, the fair market value will be substantially less than the retail value. It may actually turn out to be the wholesale value. It may be even less than this.

In many cases, the value of the merchandise is inflated by the sponsors of the contest. Naturally, they want to make their gift look as important to the contestants as possible. This inflated value is not the amount that you must put in your tax returns.

People believe that the amount you must pay taxes on is the retail value, the wholesale value, or the amount you get when you sell. None of these values are necessarily correct. What you must pay is the amount a bona fide buyer would pay if he or she bought the merchandise.

The only instances in which you can declare substantially less than the value of the item are cases where the item is custom-made, or so unique that you can't find a buyer. The couch mentioned earlier is a good example of this. Or suppose you win a mink bathing suit designed by Oleg Cassini.

Even if you decide to keep the item, you need only declare the fair market value. That is, the couch, the mink bathing suit, or any other such hard-to-sell item need not be declared at full value, even if you're a willing receiver.

This means that you have to determine what the fair market value is.

This is not especially easy. Check prices in newspapers, magazines, mail-order catalogs and direct-mail advertisements. These prices will probably not vary much. You certainly will have to research the matter very carefully.

Do you always have to pay taxes? No. Sometimes you may be the lucky winner of a contest in which the sponsors offer to pay your taxes for you. If this is the case, you must list this reimbursement on your tax forms as another source of income, and you'll end up paying taxes on the taxes!

What are deductible expenses? First of all, you can only deduct these expenses if you win. If you enter 1000 sweepstakes and win nothing, none of these items can be deducted on your tax returns. You must be a winner. In other words, your sweepstakes hobby must provide you with a source of income.

Here are some of the items you can deduct if you do win.

1: The money you spend on postage stamps.

2: The money you spend on paper, pencils, pens, index cards, stickers, address labels, pads of paper, scrap paper, paper clips, staples, dictionaries, lexicons, thesauruses, and that big calendar you bought so you could keep track of closing dates.

3: The price of any sweepstakes books you purchase.

4: The price of subscriptions to sweepstakes magazines.

5: If you should happen to win a lottery, you may deduct the price of all your losing tickets.

The IRS announced on January 30, 1973, that winners of state lotteries are eligible to deduct the cost of losing tickets against their winnings when they are listing deductions on their tax forms.

Of course, as in all other cases, this gambling loss can only be claimed if you win something!

If you bought cereal or soap, or any other product that you can actually use, you may not deduct the cost of the product. This is for two reasons—first, the product is of use, and therefore a personal expense, and second, you need not, in

many cases, actually purchase the product in order
to win. Many winners have used blank sheets of
paper and printed the name of the product in block
letters. This technique was described earlier.

Chapter Nine

ALL ABOUT LOTTERIES

Lotteries are a very recent institution in America. For many years we didn't have lotteries. People were suspicious of them. No one really believed it was possible to win something for nothing. This is one reason why many of the state lotteries did so poorly when they first were reinstituted in the United States. Also, lotteries have a long history of being exploited by private individuals—but more about this later.

The following chapters on lotteries will tell you all about lotteries, both domestic and foreign, a history of lotteries, and a rundown on some of the lotteries in the United States, how they work, and what the odds are for winning.

Also, I'm going to tell you about lotteries in other countries, but as you will see, it is not a good idea to become involved with them.

You may not believe that anyone ever wins lot-

teries, but as countless news stories will testify, there
are plenty of winners in the United States, people
lifted from middle-class and lower-class life into the
realm of ease. In some countries, the lottery is the
only chance for a really poor person to achieve
money, status, and success. It is the poor man's
dream. He may not have enough to eat, a place to
live, or a job, but he always buys a lottery ticket.

Here, the differences between rich and poor
economic strata are vast, but the poor and middle
class have at least some chance of upgrading their
economic levels. The lottery can provide this
chance. If you happen to have moral scruples
against any form of gambling, I'm certainly not
trying to sway you or convince you to change your
way of life. But even many religious organizations
accept and provide gambling of various kinds to
their followers.

This book is for those of us who have no qualms
about legal, safe, gambling.

My job is to provide you with the facts. You may
do as you wish with them.

If you should decide to enter the lottery, I wish
you the best of luck, and I certainly hope that you'll
win at least $1,000,000.

There are many winners. You might as well be
one!

What Is a Lottery?

A lottery is a way of distributing money or prizes
to a large group of people. A lottery is a form of
gambling. It combines the three elements of prize,

chance, and consideration. In government lotteries, the prizes are usually cash prizes. The element of chance means that you must depend on your good fortune to win, and that winners are selected by random drawings. The consideration present is the cost of your ticket or tickets.

In state lotteries, the values of the prizes are set at a fixed amount. Some of the money that remains pays for expenses, promotion, and so forth. What is left goes for state purposes. Some states use these funds to help pay for educational facilities.

In most very large lotteries, there is usually one very large prize and a number of smaller ones. This kind of arrangement has the psychological advantage of drawing people into the game. Everyone wants to be a millionaire, so of course, the lure is to win the big prize. But many others also win something. Often small winners stake their prizes on future lotteries.

The lottery, as I have explained, has the decided advantage of earning money for the state. It is a popular way to earn money, since many people are intrigued by the idea of entering. You may not even be a gambler at heart, but usually the cost of tickets is so slight, and your confidence in the legality so great, that you might try anyway.

Throughout its history, the lottery has been a controversial method for raising revenue.

Actually, the lottery is an ancient institution. You will find references to it in the Bible. In the Old Testament, Num. 26:55-6, the Lord tells Moses to divide land among the Israelites by lot. In ancient Rome there were Saturnalia feasts, and other famous holidays. Nero and Augustus, two powerful

Roman emperors, used lotteries during these occasions to give away land and property to upper-class Romans.

Today, lotteries have been used to draft men into the army as well as for commercial prize promotions where many gifts are given away. However, when I talk about lotteries I'm not talking about those used for military conscription or private prize promotions. In this book I will discuss only the state lotteries that cost money to enter and give away money for prizes.

In the fifteenth-century, a number of small European townships instituted lotteries to earn money for the building of fortifications and also for aiding the poor.

In France, Francis I, grandfather of Francis II who was to become the teen-aged husband of Mary, Queen of Scots, allowed his subjects to establish lotteries for both public and private profit. This was done in several French cities between 1520 and 1539.

In Florence, Italy, in 1539, *La Lotto de Firenze* was established. This was the first lottery to give away cash prizes. The idea of the lottery spread like wildfire to other cities. In 1863, the first national Italian lottery was established. This lottery had weekly drawings and was used to provide revenue to the state. The Italian National Lottery is called *Lotto*. Many modern gambling games are based on it.

In 1530, the English Queen Elizabeth I established the first public lottery in London. The money made from this lottery was used to finance harbors.

In 1612, James I allowed the Virginia Company to start a public lottery to earn money for the building of the Jamestown colony in the New World. Many businessmen had objections to this lottery, and the money supplied was far from enough to finance this costly adventure. Still, at the time, a lottery was accepted as a legitimate way to make money.

By 1621, the Virginia Company earned almost half its yearly income from the lottery, but soon there was to be so much argument within the company that the House of Commons decided to prohibit it from running any more lotteries. In 1627, a public lottery was held to finance an aqueduct in London. Lotteries were banned in England from 1699 to 1709, and again in 1826.

Why were lotteries banned? This is an interesting question because lotteries have been banned off and on in this country for the same or similar reasons. Lotteries have always been questionable institutions. It seems that throughout history, it has been almost impossible to run a lottery without some kind of fraud. Some of the problems that came about in seventeenth- and eighteenth-century England have influenced the public opinion of lotteries in that country and in this one up until the present.

For most of this period in England, lotteries were the only acceptable, legal, public form of gambling. They were advertised with much hoopla and determination. Some were even advertised with torchlight processions.

But certain private contractors would buy wholesale tickets and mark up the prices so that citizens would have to pay a lot of money for tickets that originally cost little.

A side bet developed. You might make a small bet about whether this or that ticket would be drawn from the regular lottery. Interestingly, this side bet was called insurance.

These two practices produced no money for the government. Dishonest operators, however, made a fortune. Both the government and the general populace thus became disenchanted with the lottery.

Besides, there was the moral contention that lotteries encouraged public gambling, and also there was the great fear among the common folk that drawings were not fairly conducted.

Before the lottery ban in 1826, many public and private works were financed in this manner. These included such projects as the British Museum in London and building projects in the American colonies. George Washington held a lottery to pay for the road over the Cumberland Mountains.

One of the first lotteries proposed in the United States was a lottery to pay for the Revolutionary War. This was the idea of the First Continental Congress, but the Congress decided against this plan, since by this time, most people had a great fear of lotteries and the abuses that usually developed because of them.

During a period of 30 years after this, however, many small lotteries were held to earn money for colleges including Harvard and King's College —later to be renamed Columbia University.

Lotteries were also held by small businessmen in England and America to sell products. In many cases these businessmen made more money than by regular sales. This was probably the beginning of what was later to become prize promotion in the United States, the idea of contests and sweepstakes to promote and encourage the consumption of certain products and services.

Private companies, as I have already pointed out, are not actually allowed to use lotteries for this purpose, and so they change the lottery by removing one or two of the elements that make a lottery what it is. In a sweepstakes, the element of consideration present is removed, since you don't have to pay for your lot or chance. In a contest, the element of skill replaces the element of chance.

By 1832, lotteries had become extremely popular in the United States. The *Boston Mercantile Journal* reported that 420 lotteries had been held in eight states the previous year. But since private contractors continued to misuse and abuse the lottery, by 1827 postmasters were forbidden to sell tickets. Already moves were being made to ban lotteries. Many states put through antilottery laws and in 1868 the Congress legislated that anything having to do with lotteries could not be sent through the mail. This piece of legislation included a very complete description of what could and could not be sent through the mails and was later supported by the Supreme Court.

In 1869, interestingly, after the mail legislation, a very effective lottery was established in Louisiana. This lottery ran for 25 years and it had agents in every major city in the United States. When it was doing its best, the Louisiana Lottery made as much as $2,000,000 a month. Prizes ran to $250,000 and two times a year $600,000 prizes were given away.

In 1890 (the Louisiana Lottery ran a few years longer), President Benjamin Harrison and the Congress both agreed that lotteries were swindling organizations and they prohibited the interstate transportation of tickets. One can scarcely imagine what bootlegging practices developed after this proposal was signed into law.

The Louisiana Lottery, famous for its corruption, was the last lottery in the United States until 1963. At this time New Hampshire started a lottery.

Chapter Ten

HOW DO LOTTERIES WORK?

First of all, the lottery must include a method for recording the bettor's identity and the amount he is betting. This can be done in a number of ways. In some cases the bettor submits his name, or name and address, on a ticket, the ticket is entered in a drawing, and he is notified if his ticket is drawn. In other cases, the bettor receives a ticket with a number on it. A matching ticket is submitted for the drawing. After the drawing takes place, it is the responsibility of the bettor to find out if his number was drawn. The number of tickets he buys represents the amount of money he is betting.

The numbers game is a corrupt version of the lottery and is a very popular racket in major American cities. In this case, the bettor submits a series of numbers to a professional bettor or bookie who tells him later if has won. The numbers game generally goes along with other illegal practices that come under the rubric of organized crime.

The lottery drawing is conducted in a number of ways, but usually goes something like this: tickets or countertickets are collected and pooled. The tickets are shaken in a container. Chance completely determines which tickets are drawn. Sometimes it's convenient to use a computer since computers have large and accurate memories and are good at picking random numbers for winners. The use of the computer further insures the element of chance in the drawings.

The illegal numbers racket works differently. One method of payoff might be based on the winnings of horses at several tracks and the sum used as a winning number. Another method would be to use the first three digits of the total amount of shares traded on the stock exchange. The numbers are usually obtained from published figures, so in some cases, if you know the method being used, it's possible to discover the winning numbers before you place your bet.

The Irish Sweepstakes is a particularly exciting game of chance. In this Sweepstakes, there are two drawings. One drawing determines the winning numbers. In another drawing, the numbers are given to horses to decide the order of the prizes.

The money earned by lotteries is collected and banked. In some national lotteries a method for the benefit of the poor has been instituted. Tickets are divided into fractions, so a person may actually buy a fraction of a ticket, and place a bet at a reduced rate. The stakes are small enough for the very poor to enter. Also, in many countries the mails are used to pass along information about lotteries, but in the United States, as stated before, there are very strict regulations on what may be sent through the mail.

First of all, the government has to decide the frequency of the lottery, and the size of the prizes. At different times throughout the year, the actual amount of the prizes may differ, as may the cost of the tickets. The costs of promotion are deducted from the total amount of money collected, and also the cost of the prizes. The money that remains is retained by the state. In most cases, something like 50 to 60 percent of the pooled money goes back to the winners.

The amount and distribution of the prizes is a weighty psychological factor determining the success of state lotteries. Prizes may be big or small, equal or unequal. Usually, the lottery gets a particularly good response if there is at least one very large prize. If this is so, every entrant has the hope of winning it. Usually the large prize is backed up by a number of smaller prizes which winners may, in fact, spend on the lottery next time around.

For instance, if someone wins $100 in the lottery, he may turn around and buy $100 worth of tickets in the next lottery. He has increased his chances of winning the big prize several times over.

Remember, just as in sweepstakes or contests, the more often you enter the better are your chances of winning. In other words, if you buy 1 ticket and there are 1,000,000 tickets all together, you have 1 chance out of 1,000,000 of winning. If you buy 200 tickets out of 1,000,000 tickets, you have increased your chances of winning by 199 times.

Where are there lotteries today? Just about everywhere. There are lotteries in Africa, the Near East, Europe, some Communist countries, many Latin American countries, Japan, and Australia. There are lotteries in a few countries of Asia. The People's Republic of China, however, forbids lotteries. They are also forbidden in India.

For many years in Soviet Russia lotteries were illegal, but now even there they are legal. Only private gambling is illegal.

Australia has the biggest and best state lottery, however. All states are involved except South Australia, and in New South Wales, they sell up to 1,000,000 tickets a week.

Why aren't there lotteries in every country?

There is still considerable resistance in many places. In England there have been countless attempts to institute a form of lottery, and countless failures. There have been many debates, and countless numbers of bills have been rejected. One reason for this is that there are many other forms of public gambling in England, and the government is not anxious to provide more.

In 1967 the complaint was voiced by many that England was a gambler's paradise. The British working class has soccer pools and raffles, and bingo is also very popular. Also you can buy bonds, which I will explain later.

Many people feel that institutionalized gambling reduces the interest in gambling. Others feel that it only adds to the total number of possibilities for gambling.

Chapter Eleven

WHO WINS STATE LOTTERIES?

Anybody can win a lottery. That's what this book is all about.

In 1968, a 16-month-old baby named Frederick Maurice Mizrahi earned himself $100,000 by having a ticket placed for him in a state lottery.

In 1967, Anis Hamway, 62 years old and a Jordanian immigrant, paid $1 for tickets and won $100,000. He's keeping the money for his son's education which means the son could go through Harvard five or six times, depending on inflation. And, Mr. Hamway still works in his grocery store from 5:00 a.m. to 9:00 p.m.

Mrs. Hannah Hendry was married three days when she learned she was a winner of the lottery. She was on her honeymoon at the time. She and her husband came right back home and eventually settled in East Orange, New Jersey.

Charles Holt, a university student, won the lottery. He considered his prize a windfall; It meant that he could get married before he expected.

A Roman Catholic school in Patterson, New Jersey, won $100,000 in the New Jersey State Lottery, and used the money to buy a much needed gymnasium for its 700 students.

Then there was the bartender who signed his ticket, "W. Dopie."

Joseph Bonasia, 49 years old and a police detective, won $100,000. He was painting his house when his wife told him the good news. He stopped painting only long enough to kiss her. He continues to work at his $11,000-a-year job.

The newlywed Mrs. Lena Caputo, 21 years old, was able, because of her $100,000 winnings, to join her husband who was a soldier in West Germany.

One winner in the New Jersey State Lottery, a man named Doug Berstler, picked nine winning tickets in a two-year period. These winning tickets were for smaller prizes, but his total winnings amounted to $220,000.

Although the lottery office calculated that the odds against winning that many times in that short a period were something like 75 million to 1, Mr. Berstler didn't find his good fortune remarkable. He thought he had worked out a system.

Apparently his first son was born on a Friday the 13th, so he was always careful to choose tickets with 13 in the number. Also he only bought tickets from local stores that hadn't recently had a winner. He felt they were due to win. He almost always bought his tickets the night before the drawing.

This system probably wouldn't work for anyone

else. The lottery office felt it was really a matter of Mr. Berstler's incredible good fortune, although his lucky breaks with the lottery were preceded by other unfortunate events. He had lost his job because the gas station he operated closed down due to the gasoline shortage. And his house burned down because of a faulty electrical circuit.

He used some of the money to rebuild his house. Also he took his family on a much-needed vacation. The rest of the money he decided to save for the college education of his four children.

In October of 1973, Mrs. Dorothy Lavers discovered a batch of lottery tickets in the garbage of her son's best friend. These tickets were already two weeks old, but among them was a winner—number 954, the winner of the previous week's drawing.

Sometimes out-of-state people win the lottery. This happened in January of 1974 when Mrs. Hazel H. Johnston of St. Louis won the 32nd New Jersey Millionaire lottery. So if you don't have a lottery in your state, you can buy tickets from other state lotteries. You have as good a chance of winning as the residents of that state.

How do people respond when they learn that they are winners of the lottery?

In March of 1974 a man who was a freight conductor on a railroad won $1,000,000 in the New Jersey State Lottery. He said that it was "the Lord's will," and that he planned to "spread the Gospel of the Lord." He would receive $50,000 a year for the next 20 years.

Other winners have been surprisingly nonchalant when they heard of their good fortune. A 75-year-old semi retired detective said, "I suppose some people would be thrilled." He certainly didn't seem to be. Another winner of $100,000 said, "It feels okay."

It seems that the winners of big money quickly discover the problems of getting rich fast. First there is the big tax bite. Some winners complain that they lose as much as 70 percent of their winnings. Also the winners receive calls from all kinds of salesmen and cranks demanding money. One not so lucky winner swears that every time he went out in the street, strangers ran up to him and tried to touch him. They hoped that some of his good luck would rub off on them.

Many people don't really understand how to manage their newfound wealth. One New Jersey tailor immediately removed the sign from his shop and decided to retire for life.

One couple who won $1,000,000 in the state lottery became so frightened by public acclaim that they barred the press from their house. The wife developed an ulcer.

Another couple, the happy winners of $200,000, ran off to California where they spent everything and returned almost penniless.

One winner hoped that his winnings would be the answer to all his prayers, but he sadly remarked that he had the same problems, the same hang-ups, that he had before he got rich. Money doesn't solve everything, after all.

Most individuals and their families are very cautious with their winnings. In New Jersey, 30 winners of the lottery formed a Millionaire's Club where they discuss the problems of being rich—how to invest, what to do with the money, the temptations of wild spending, and other problems.

The millionaires help each other with many important decisions, such as whether or not one or another of them should change their job or their lifestyle. The club members manage to calm each other down and help each other from spending unwisely. They meet four times a year for dinner and dancing.

Many of these millionaires are afraid that their sudden wealth and notoriety will spoil their family lives.

The Tilton family in New Jersey was a typical winning family faced with this problem. It seems that after winning they did everything they could to preserve their family as it was, and to maintain their lifestyle.

For one thing, they were reluctant to sell their house. Dick Tilton had built it. It was a two-story frame house on a 100-by-100-foot plot. Besides, Mr. and Mrs. Tilton were reluctant to move because their kids had friends in the neighborhood and at their school, and naturally they didn't want to part with them.

Within a week after winning, the family had received letters from investment firms and real estate people, congratulatory calls, and calls from beggars. They had to change their phone to an unlisted number.

Patsy bought herself a new car with air conditioning to replace her battered 1963 Ford.

Dick didn't want to stop working. He liked his job. He was a civil electronics technician at the Army's Electronics Command at Fort Monmouth, New Jersey. When he went to work after the drawing, he found that his pals had painted his phone gold, and had spread paper money all over his desk top. When he arrived, they made him sit down and stuck a cigar in his mouth.

Patsy Tilton was particularly worried about the effect their big winnings would have on the kids. She was worried not only because she felt certain it would change their lives, but also because of moral reasons. She had always tried to teach the children that you can't get something for nothing. And here they were, big winners in the lottery.

During the first week, she found it important to keep their schedules the same as before. She took them to the beach club every day, a club to which the family had belonged before. She felt it was relaxing for herself, and kept the children with friends.

Six months after the drawing, the Tiltons have begun to accumulate a few tokens of newfound wealth. They have a pair of dashing cars in the driveway, one a dark brown Oldsmobile, the other a bright red Pontiac. They also bought wall-to-wall carpeting for their house.

The family took a one-week vacation on a dude ranch, and bought Western clothes to outfit themselves. Everyone in the family has padded out their wardrobe. Still there has been no rash spending.

The kids still receive modest presents for birthdays and Christmas—Brownie uniforms, tennis rackets and lessons, sleeping bags, tape recorders. Patsy is very afraid that they will feel different from the other kids, and she is doing everything she can to prevent this from happening.

The Tiltons are both happy and depressed. It's nice to be able to pay all the bills on time, but Dick doesn't feel as much like one of the boys as he used to. He dislikes the constant joking at the office.

They have also joined the Millionaire's Club in order to discuss their newfound wealth and new problems.

Winning a million can be as frightening as it is wonderful. Especially if you have little experience with investing—and with fame. Nobody wants crank calls and nobody wants to be touched and bothered on the street.

But still, with all that money—well, if you don't let it go to your head, you can probably find a way to enjoy yourself. You can always get advice from other big winners, or join an organization like the Millionaire's Club.

Chapter Twelve

WHICH STATES HAVE LOTTERIES?

If you don't have a lottery in your state and you are interested in buying lottery tickets, you'll first probably want to find out about the lotteries in other states, how they work, and how you can enter. You'll want to write to the lotteries of each state that interests you, find out about closing dates, what the prizes are, and how you can find out if your number has been drawn.

The U.S. Post Office is very fussy about any correspondence that has to do with lotteries, so it's best for you if you send your letters first-class mail. Don't use postcards—postcards may seem simpler to you, but your chances of getting a response are not good.

Use a plain sheet of white paper, keep your letter brief, make sure you include all the questions above, write neatly or type, make sure you put enough postage on the envelope, and include your zip code.

Date all your lottery letters, and keep a copy of each. The copy is for your records. It will help you to keep track of which lotteries you are interested in, and the ones for which you have requested information.

In your letter you should ask for all available information about the lottery. Find out what kind of lottery is being played, and find out how you can buy tickets. Ask for any brochures that might be available.

Allow plenty of time for your request to reach the lottery and plenty of time for a response. You may be in a hurry, but remember, most lotteries have drawings every month, and some have them weekly. There's plenty of time for you to become a millionaire.

How can you find out the latest news about lotteries, and how can you find out what the winning numbers are?

There's a publication called *Lottery Parlay Magazine* that covers all the news about both domestic and foreign lotteries. This magazine is an excellent publication for anyone who is interested in entering lotteries.

The magazine can tell you which states are running lotteries. It tells about special drawings, what people are doing with their prizes, and about new lotteries, how they are being set up, how they are being run, and how to buy tickets for them.

If you are interested in subscribing to this magazine, write to *Lottery Parlay Magazine,* Box 7288, Philadelphia, Pennsylvania 19101.

Ask for information about the magazine, subscription rates, and make sure you include your own name, address and zip code for return mail.

To date there are currently 11 state lotteries (listed here in order of gross sales for 1974): Michigan, Pennsylvania, Massachusetts, New Jersey, Illinois, Ohio, Maryland, Connecticut, Rhode Island, New Hampshire and Maine. Delaware dropped its first effort in the lottery business but is polishing up a replacement. The Omaha City Council voted for one last spring, and Washington, D.C., Virginia and South Carolina are considering their own. As recently as 1970 only two states had lotteries. The trend is obvious.

Here is a description of a few of the state lotteries, how they work, and how the games are played.

Illinois:

The Illinois game depends on a lot of excitement and big money. They have what they refer to as a numbers game. The success of the game depends on three factors: a large number of winners, attractive, large prizes, and simple rules.

The way the Illinois lottery keeps people interested is by having many small drawings weekly as well as the large millionaire prizes. This has the psychological advantage that I've talked about before—everyone wants to be a millionaire, but the small prizes give players a chance to invest a little more money and try again.

The Illinois lottery also keeps the cost of its tickets low.

For more information, write to: Illinois Lottery Commission, State Capitol Building, Springfield, Illinois 62706. Phone: 217/782-6472.

Connecticut:

Connecticut has a weekly game and a super weekly game. This state does not have a millionaire game. In the weekly game, one winning number is on each 50-cent ticket. If the weekly number is 12345:

xx345 wins	$20
x234x wins	$20
123xx wins	$20
Scramble (any combination of winning digits)	$25
x2345 wins	$200
1234x wins	$200
12345 wins	$500

In order to enter the super weekly game, you must be a $5000 winner. To enter, you must register your claim at an authorized claim center.

If the regular lottery sells at least 1,000,000 tickets, the following week a super-weekly will be held, and winners who have registered their claims the week before will be notified.

Besides the $100,000 prize, prizes of $15,000 are also given away.

For information about subscriptions, brochures, prizes, and how to enter, write: Connecticut State Lottery Commission on Special Revenue, Box 224, 176 Cumberland Avenue, Weathersfield, Connecticut 06107. Phone: 203/566-2912.

Maryland:

On a Maryland lottery ticket there are two numbers, one a 6-digit number, the other a 5-digit millionaire's finalist number. Each ticket costs 50 cents.

In the weekly game, if the weekly number is 123456:

xx34xx wins	$5
123xxx wins	$25
xxx456 wins	$25
1234xx wins	$100
xx3456 wins	$100
12345x wins	$1000
x23456 wins	$1000
123456 wins	$50,000

Every week after the regular drawing, another drawing is held to determine the millionaire finalist number. If you have this number, you must register your claim at one of the 300 claim centers. At various intervals, millionaire drawings are held.

For more information about the Maryland State Lottery, write to: Maryland State Lottery Agency, The Rotunda, 711 West 40th Street, Baltimore, Maryland 21211. Phone: 301/383-6311.

New Jersey:

The New Jersey lottery has a daily game, a weekly game, and a millionaire game. Daily tickets cost 50 cents and have a 5-digit number on them. The weekly tickets also cost 50 cents and have a 6-digit number on them.

In the daily game, if the number is 12345:

xx345 wins	$25
x234x wins	$25
123xx wins	$25

A 5-digit scramble or any combination of the winning 5 digits in any order wins $25

x2345 wins	$225
1234x wins	$225
54321 wins	$1000
12345 wins	$10,000

All losing daily tickets are automatically entered into a grand drawing where winning tickets are chosen for a top prize of $75,000 and other smaller prizes of $5000 each. The grand drawing is held every week after the weekly drawing on Thursday morning each time a total of 3.6 million daily tickets are sold. Finalists' tickets are placed in a ball which is spun. Then 6 tickets are chosen, and each finalist is given a post position at the track. The winning horse determines the winning grand-prize number, and the other five following winning positions receive the remaining $5000 prizes.

In the weekly game, if the number is 123456:

123xxx wins	$25
xxx456 wins	$25
1234xx wins	$250
xx3456 wins	$250
12345x wins	$2500
x23456 wins	$2500
654321 wins	$5000
123456 wins	$50,000

The last single digit of your number qualifies you for the millionaire game. If you are a finalist, you must register at once. Millionaire drawings are held at various intervals.

For more information, write to: New Jersey State Lottery Commission, State Capitol, Trenton, New Jersey. Phone: 609/292-4331.

New Hampshire:

New Hampshire had the first lottery to be reinstituted in the United States after the Louisiana Lottery was banned many years ago.

New Hampshire does not have a millionaire game. Instead it has what is called a Hundred Grand Super Draw Game. Otherwise, this state has a regular weekly game in which a 5-digit number appears on each 50-cent weekly ticket.

If the number in the weekly game is 12345:

xx345 wins	$20
123xx wins	$20
1234x wins	$200

A 5-digit scramble or any combination of the winning 5 digits in any order wins $20

x2345 wins	$200
12345 wins	$5000

If the last digit of your ticket matches the last digit of the winning number, then deposit your ticket for a possible $10 win. Every week that 100,000 tickets are sold, 75 such winners are drawn.

In the Super Draw, all winners are eligible, but must register their claims immediately.

After 1,000,000 have been sold, eight semifinalists are chosen from the winners' pool.

The following week, a Super Draw is held and the eight semifinalists receive prizes of $2500, $5000 and the finalist's prize of $100,000.

Also, New Hampshire has a weekly game called the Lucky Dollar Game. You purchase a Lucky Dollar ticket for $1. On your ticket there will be two numbers, one 3-digit number, and one 5-digit number. If the numbers drawn match any of the numbers on your ticket, you win the amount in cash adjacent to your winning number.

If your number matches one of the Lifetime Finalist numbers, you may enter the Lifetime drawing. The first eight finalists win $5000 in cash. The next finalist wins $10,000. And the last finalist wins $500 in cash every month for life, with a guaranteed total of no less than $200,000.

Drawings in the Lucky Dollar game are held just about once every five weeks. Claim centers in New Hampshire are liquor stores, race tracks, or the Sweepstakes Commission Office. Subscriptions are available.

For information write: New Hampshire Sweepstakes Commission, 125 Main Street, Concord, New Hampshire 03301. Phone: 603/271-3391.

Michigan:

The Michigan lottery includes three games, a weekly drawing followed by a Super Draw and a Million Dollar Game. Your 50-cent weekly ticket has a double 3-digit number on it.

In the weekly game if the number is 123 456:

123 xxx wins	$25
xxx 456 wins	$25
xxx 123 wins	$25
456 xxx wins	$25

123 456 is eligible for the Super Draw
456 123 is eligible for the Super Draw

If you qualify for the Super Draw, you must register your claim. In the Super Draw, the top prize is $200,000. There is one prize of $25,000; one prize of $15,000; one prize of $12,500; one prize of $10,000; and one prize of $5000. The winner of the $5000 prize can return the following week and try for the top prize.

In the Million Dollar Game, all $25 weekly winners who clamed their winnings will receive a check with a number on it. After 120,000 people have won and claimed their $25 prizes and checks, a computer selects 120 finalists. Every finalist gets at least $1,000 and 1 person gets $1,000,000.

The Michigan lottery has subscriptions. Find out where claim centers are from the person who sells you tickets.

For information write: Michigan Bureau of State Lottery, 940 Long Boulevard, Lansing, Michigan 48913. Phone: 517/373-6350.

Rhode Island:

Rhode Island has a weekly game. Each 50-cent ticket is divided into three color-coded sections: blue, green and gold.

The blue section has five 3-digit numbers, so you have five chances to match exactly the winning blue number and win a $20 prize. For every 1,000,000 tickets sold, there are 5000 matches.

The green section has five 6-digit numbers listed. If your first number matches, you win $50,000. If your second number matches, you win $10,000. If any of the last three numbers match, you win $5000.

For every 1,000,000 tickets sold there is one match for each of these five numbers.

The gold section has five 6-digit numbers, so you have five chances to match the winning number for a $2000 prize, and each winning number qualifies for the $200,000 Super Draw. For every 1,000,000 tickets sold, there are five matches.

In the Super Draw, 20 gold winners from the last five to seven weeks compete for a grand prize of $200,000, a second prize of $10,000, and a third of $5000.

For information write: Rhode Island State Lottery Agency, State Capitol Building, Providence, Rhode Island. Phone: 401/438-7900.

Chapter Thirteen

WHAT ARE THE ODDS?

In the Connecticut weekly game, your odds of winning a weekly prize ranging from $25 to $5000 are 1 in 274. The odds of winning the super prize of $75,000 are 1 in 1,000,000.

In the Michigan weekly game, your odds are 1 in 250 of winning any prize, ranging from $25 to $1,000,000. Your chances of winning the $1,000,000 prize are 1 in 30,000,000; chances of winning $100,000 are 1 in 29,999,999, chances of winning $50,000 are 1 in 29,999,999. Chances of winning $25 are 1 in 1,000, chances of winning $27,500 are 1 in 500,000, chances of winning $5000 are 1 in 4,857,714 and your chances of winning $1000 are 1 in 272,727.

In Pennsylvania's weekly game, your chances of winning any prize are 1 in 526. Your chances of winning $50,000 are 1 in 1,000,000. Your chances of making it to the millionaire game are 1 in

100,000 and your chances of becoming a millionaire are 1 in 30,000,000.

In Pennsylvania's Lucky Seven game, you have 1 in 167 chances of winning any prize. Odds range from 1 in 1,000,000 for the top $75,000-prize to 1 in 1,004 for the low $50-prize. In the Baker's Dozen, you have 1 in 247 chances of winning any prize. Odds range from 1 in 1,000,000 for the top $100,000 prize to 1 in 1,000 for the $25 prize.

In the New Jersey weekly, your chances of winning any prize are 1 in 500. Odds range from 1 in 1,000,000 for the top $50,000-prize to 1 in 1111 for the bottom $25 prize. In the millionaire game, your odds are 1 in 20,000,000 for the top prize. They are 1 in 19,999,999 for the second, third, and fourth prizes.

In the New Jersey daily, your chances of winning any prize are 1 in 27. The odds of winning the top prize of $2500 are 1 in 100,000 and the bottom prize of $2.50 are 1 in 111.

In the Massachusetts weekly, your chances of winning a prize are 1 in 500. Odds are 1 in 1,000,-000 for the top $50,000 prize. You have 1 chance in 100,000 to make the $1,000,000 drawing, and your chances of winning the $1,000,000 prize are 1 in 12,000,000.

Generally speaking, between 40 to 50 percent of the money collected is returned in the form of prizes to winners. Odds are always greater for the largest prizes.

What If You Win?

At one point some $11,000,000 won in the state lotteries was unclaimed by winners. New Jersey

estimated that about $3,000,000 was going un-
claimed, Maryland estimated about $1,000,000,
Pennsylvania estimated about $3,000,000, Con-
necticut estimated about $500,000. Estimates of
these and other states added up to about
$11,000,000.

So if you enter the lottery, make sure always to
check your numbers against the winning numbers,
and if you have entered a lottery in which any of a
series of digits win, check your numbers, the order
of the digits, and so forth. You may have a winner,
and not know it—like the young man who threw
his tickets in the garbage, these same tickets to be
discovered later by a neighbor. In most lotteries, it's
not just a single number that wins, but often, part of
the winning number wins something, and sometimes a scrambled number wins.

That's why it's so important to understand the
rules of each lottery that you enter.

Here are the three cardinal rules of winning in
state lotteries.

1. Enter often.
2. Understand the rules.
3. Always check your number against the winning numbers.

If you happen to have old tickets lying around
and you're unsure of them, write to the state lottery
agency and ask if these numbers were winners. It
wouldn't do any harm to make certain. And you
might, even now, be a winner and not know it.

You may also be asking, what about taxes? Let
me just say a couple of things. (See Chapter Eight
also.)

First, sometimes as much as 70 percent of your
winnings go to taxes, and of course, the bigger your

winnings, the more taxes you pay. That's why in the millionaire games, you collect your winnings over a number of years. This reduces the giant tax bite, and provides you with a steady and very substantial income over a number of years.

If you're worried about taxes or have any questions that you can't seem to find answers to, get in touch with the Internal Revenue Service or a tax expert who can tell you what deductions and claims you are allowed to make.

Chapter Fourteen

FOREIGN LOTTERIES

The United States government takes a dim view of its citizens entering foreign lotteries. The official policy is that you cannot enter. Besides, something like 75 percent of all foreign lottery tickets sold in this country are counterfeit, so you might as well save your effort. Another fact is that the statistics are not in your favor, and your chances of winning, even if your ticket is good, are much fewer than your chances of winning a domestic lottery.

But if you feel you really want to give the foreign lotteries a try, see if you can get copies of *International Lottery Magazine*. Send an airmail letter to: A.J.M. Kriek, *International Lottery Magazine*, Salviahof 26, Noordwijk Binnen, The Netherlands. Check with the Post Office to find out what the cost of postage is to The Netherlands.

In your letter, give Mr. Kriek your name, address

and zip code. Ask about the magazine and how much it will cost.

Following are some of the major foreign lotteries now in existence and brief descriptions of how they work.

England:

England doesn't really have a lottery as such. Instead they have what is called a National Savings Bond. If you buy one of these bonds, you have a lifetime ticket in the lottery.

What happens is the British government pays no interest on the bonds to bondholders, but each month pays 4¾ percent interest on all the bonds to a prize fund. Drawings are held to determine winners and the amount of your winnings depends on the amount of interest you have in the fund at the time.

Drawings are held on a weekly and monthly basis and prizes range from $65 to $130,000. You buy bonds at the Post Office and your name is entered on a permanent basis. Once you own a bond, you participate in every drawing.

If you are a citizen of the United States you may buy a bond, but there are some difficulties involved. First of all, you cannot buy a bond through the mail. You may buy it either on a trip to England or you may have a friend buy it for you.

The U.S. Post Office won't permit gambling information to pass through the mails. Thus, when drawings are held you won't be notified if you reside in the United States. You must either have a British friend check the drawings for you, or you must check yourself on a subsequent trip to England.

Irish Sweepstakes:

As unlikely as it seems, many people still enter and win money in the Irish Sweepstakes.

This lottery is illegal in the United States, yet as much as $30,000,000 are spent on it annually by United States citizens. Postal inspectors, the U.S. Treasury, the FBI, as well as state and local police are all out to stop the importation of Irish Sweepstakes tickets into the United States, but it seems that most of their efforts have failed.

The Sweepstakes still thrives.

Today, however, because of the legalized state lotteries, many former Sweepstakes ticket agents have turned legitimate. To some, it's simply not worth the risk of getting caught. Only a dozen or more years ago, an Irish freighter was invaded by U.S. Customs officials who found 50 crates of illegal Irish Sweepstakes tickets.

One reason why the Sweepstakes is so popular in the United States is probably because the drawings are so colorful, and the stakes are very good if you should happen to win. One New Jerseyite in 1967 won the first-prize money of $224,000. He won again the following year a prize of $131,796.

However, if you plan to enter the Irish Sweepstakes, you must beware of counterfeit tickets. A counterfeiter obtains an honest ticket and an honest receipt. He then makes plates and simply prints off copies of this ticket and receipt. He then sells his copies to a legitimate dealer usually for wholesale prices.

Australia:

Every year the ticket sales for the Australian Lottery amount to some $60,000,000. If you are a U.S. citizen, your checks, bank drafts, and money orders will be accepted by the State Lottery Authorities in each city, but the U.S. Postal Service has the right to stop mail addressed to foreign lotteries. Sometimes they do and sometimes they don't.

For information about the New South Wales Lottery, write to Director of State Lotteries, Box 4321, G.P.O., Sydney, N.S.W. 2001, Australia.

In the ordinary lottery, major prizes range from $18,000 to $1050. Minor prizes amount to $300, $150, $120, $90, $30, and $15. A ticket costs 82 cents.

In the special lottery, prizes range from $36,000 to $750 and the cost of the ticket is $1.50.

In the Jackpot, there are three major prizes of $90,000, $18,000, and $9,000; the Jackpot prize is $12,000, and the consolation prizes are $1,500 for tickets one number off the first prize-winning number.

In the Opera House Lottery, prizes range from $300,000 to $15,000. There are also minor prizes.

There's an ordinary and special lottery with tickets costing 75 cents and $1.50 respectively. Prizes range from $24,000 to $7.50 in the ordinary; from $45,000 to $15 in the special. There are also super-specials that are run throughout the year.

For information about the Western Australia Lottery write: G.P.O. Box C 106, Perth, Western Australia, 6001, Australia.

In Queensland write to: Golden Casket Art

Union, Jackma House, 247 Adelaide Street, Brisbane, Queensland, 4000, or GPO Box 551, Brisbane, Queensland, 4001, Australia.

Major prizes in the ordinary lottery range from $22,000 to $900, minor prizes from $300 to $15. Tickets cost 90 cents.

In the Treasure Chest, major prizes range from $45,000 to $600 and minor prizes range from $300 to $30. Tickets cost $1.50.

There is also a Sunshine Special with a $3-ticket cost, a Monmouth Lottery with a top prize of $150,000, and, of course, the Melbourne Cup Special and Christmas Gift with a top prize of $300,000. Tickets cost $7.50.

For the Tattersall Sweep Sonsulation, write to: L. Day, P.O. Box 1682-P, GPO Melbourne, Victoria, 3001, Australia. Tickets cost 90 cents and prizes range from $37,000 to $15.

Canada:

Canadian lotteries were legalized by Parliamentary action in 1969 and today boast an average of 60 percent return on sales. In other words, the government keeps 40 percent and gives away 60 percent. To date there are six provincially run lotteries in existence with Quebec running four, Ontario one, and Manitoba one. A seventh is in the final planning stages combining the four western provinces.

The most grandiose of the above is the Olympic Lottery initiated in December of 1973 to run through the 1976 Olympics with the sole purpose of financing or helping to finance the cost of the

Olympic Games. Originally there were to be six drawings (because of the success of the lottery, additional drawings have been held and are planned) at a cost of $10 per ticket with a $1,000,-000 tax-free top prize. This is one of the four lotteries run by the province of Quebec.

On May 15, 1973, Ontario started a biweekly lottery (run by Ontario Lottery Corporation) with tickets costing $1 and drawings held every other Thursday for a grand prize of $100,000 and a variety of lesser prizes. This lottery is known as the Wintario Lottery.

Manitoba initiated its Manitoba Golden Sweepstakes in 1971. It has three drawings a year with a top prize of $150,000.

Loto Quebec is the other Quebec lottery which is divided into weekly, monthly, and quarterly drawings all based on the programs of the Swedish Lottery drawings. See breakdown of ticket costs and prizes on page 121.

The proposed Western Provinces Lottery being set up by the Western Canada Lottery Foundation will have four drawings a year. The tickets will sell for $2.50 for a top prize of $250,000.

Canadian lottery tickets can be legally sold and/ or purchased in other parts of the world, e.g., the United States, but must be collected in Canada and of course winnings are taxable upon entry into home country.

Since the United States government is opposed to citizens purchasing foreign lottery tickets, I don't advise entering foreign lotteries. But, I have nonetheless made a list of some foreign lotteries and where to write for information for anyone who wants to have a friend overseas buy tickets.

NAME OF LOTTERIES	MINI	INTER	SUPER
Frequency	Weekly	Monthly	Quarterly
Cost	50¢	$2.00	$4.00
No. of tickets sold: (estimated)	1½ m/week	1,000,000/month	500,000/season
No. of winners: (estimated)	1500/week	1000/month	500/season
Value of prizes/drawing (estimated)	$290,000 app.	$560,000 app.	$685,000 app.
Value of the first prize:	$5000 (app. 17 in number)	$125,000	$200,000
Total annual value of prizes:	$13 million app.	$7 million app.	$2 million app.
Winners per tickets sold:	1/1000	1/1000	1/1000
Drawing dates:	Every Friday at noon	Toward the tenth of the following month	Sept. 21—Dec. 21 March 21—June 21

Source: Canadian Government

ARGENTINE REPUBLIC
Loteria de Beneficiencia
Nacional Y Casinos
Santiago del Estero 126
Capital Federal, Argentina

AUSTRIA
Oesterreichische Glueck-
spielmonopolver waltung
Dominikanerbastei 16,
A-1010 Wien
Austria

BELGIUM
Loterie Nationale
12 Boulevard St. Lazare
1030, Bruxelles, Belgium

BOLIVIA
Loteria Nacional
Av., Mariscal Sta., Cruz
La Paz, Bolivia

BRAZIL
Loteria Esportiva
Superintendencia de Loterias
208 Rua do Riachuelo,
ZC 06
Rio de Janeiro, GB-20.000
Brazil

BURMA
Burma Lottery Department
27th Street
Rangoon, Burma

CEYLON
The Chairman
National Lottery Board
Galle Road, Colombo 3
Sri Lanka, Ceylon

COSTA RICA
Junta de Proteccion de Social
de San Jose
San Jose, Costa Rica

DENMARK
Finansministeriet
Christiansborg Slotsplads
1218 Copenhagen K,
Denmark

ENGLAND
Vernons Ltd.
Vermail House
Ormskirk Road
Liverpool 9, England

FINLAND
Oy veikkaus Ab,
Albertinkatu 30
00120 Helsinki 12,
Finland

FRANCE
Loterie Nationale
20 Rue La Boetie
Paris 8ieme, France

GRAND DUCHY OF
LUXEMBOURG
Loterie Nationale
35 rue Notre Dame
Luxembourg City,
G.D. of Luxembourg

GUYANA'
National Lottery Office
230 Camp Street—
Cummingsburg
Georgetown, Guyana

HONDURAS
Loteria Nacional de
Beneficencia
4a., Calle y 3a, Avenida
Tegucigalpa, D.C.,
Honduras

ISRAEL
National Lottery
3 Heftman Street
Tel Aviv, Israel

ITALY
Ministero Delle Finanze
Direzione Generale per le
Entrate Speciali
Ispettorato Generale per il
lotto e le Lotterie
Viale America
00100 Roma, Italy

IVORY COAST
Monsieur le Directeur de la
Loterie Nationale
Abidjan, Ivory Coast
West Africa

MALTA
Director of Public Lotto
74 Old Bakety Street
Valletta, Malta

MAURITIUS
The Financial Secretary
Ministry of Finance
Port-Louis, Mauritius

MEXICO
Loteria Nacional para la
Asistencia Publica
Plaza de La Reforma No. 1
Mexico, D.F., Mexico

NETHERLANDS
Stichting de Nationale
Sporttotalisator
PO Box 685,
The Hague, Netherlands

NORWAY
Det Norske Pengelotteri
Storgaten 25,
Oslo 1, Norway

PANAMA
Loteria Nacional de
Beneficencia
Apertado 21
Panama City, Panama

PARAGUAY
Loteria Paraguaya
Cerro Cora 726 c/Antequera
Asuncion, Paraguay

PORTUGAL
Santa Casa de Misericordia
Largo de Trindade Coelho
Lisbon, 2, Portugal

SINGAPORE REPUBLIC
Singapore Pools (Pte) Ltd.
219-229 Columbo Court
Singapore 6

SPAIN
Servicio National de Loterias
Guzman el Bueno, 125
Madrid, 3, Spain

SWEDEN
AB Svenska Penninglotteriet
Box 7033
S-103 81, Stockholm 7
Sweden

SWITZERLAND
International Landes—
Lotterie
Nuchelerstasse 45
CH-8001, Zurich,
Switzerland

Seva—Lotteriebureau
Muhlemattstrasse 68
CH-3007, Bern, Switzerland

Société de la Loterie de la
Suisse Romande
rue Marterey 15
CH-1005, Lausanne,
Switzerland

TRINIDAD and TOBAGO
Trinidad & Tobago
Television Co.
11 A Maraval Road
Port of Spain
Trinidad & Tobago,
West Indies

TUNISIA
Loterie Nationale
Tunisiènne
76, Avenue Farhat Hached
Tunis, Tunisia

TURKEY
Milli Piyango Genel
Mudurlugu, Ankara, Turkey

Chapter Fifteen

BINGO

Bingo is one form of gambling that is so popular throughout the country, and for some reason so acceptable, that even religious organizations promote it.

In New York City various bingo halls have opened. These are usually leased to religious groups who, for a time, organize and run the games to earn money. The major appeal seems to be to the elderly.

In a Manhattan bingo parlor, one very serious old man sits with two hot dogs in front of him and plays 32 cards at a time.

In the same parlor, a woman and her sister-in-law discuss variations of the game. The upside-down T game has produced controversy. These two women dislike the game because it's hard to win. There must be two rows filled, the vertical middle row and the bottom horizontal row.

Bingo games offer prizes that range anywhere

from a couple of dollars to expensive cars. The stiffer the competition, the bigger will be the prizes.

Sometimes religious organizations and charities expect big winners to donate some of the prize money to their coffers, but these organizations profit whether or not a donation takes place. You have to pay for each card that you play, and the sponsor profits off the money you pay.

In many cases, you are allowed to pick your own cards. If you are playing in this kind of a game, it's wise to arrive early.

This is how the cards work:

B— 1 through 15
I—16 through 30
N—31 through 45
G—46 through 60
O—61 through 75

Each card contains all the letters and some of the 75 numbers in the game. The object is to complete vertical, horizontal, and diagonal lines on your card. As each number is called, you check your card to see if you have that number, and if you do, you cover it with a chip. If you win, your card will be checked at the end of the game.

Here's how you can increase your chances of winning.

The Percentage Method

Under the letter "B" there are 15 numbers ranging from 1 through 15. Since there are 9 single numbers and only 6 double ones, your chances of having a single number called are 1½ times greater.

Under the letter "I," there are numbers ranging from 16 through 30. There are only 4 numbers in the teens and 1 number 30. There are 10 numbers in the 20s, so you should choose a card with as many numbers in the 20s as possible.

Under the letter "N" there is a free box, which increases the odds. The numbers under "N" range from 31 through 45. There are 9 numbers in the 30s, and 6 numbers in the 40s. Your chances of getting called are 1½ times greater if you have a card with most of the numbers in the 30s.

Under the letter "G," you should choose a card with numbers in the 50s. Numbers under this letter range from 46 through 60. There are 4 numbers in the 40s, 1 in the 60s and the rest are in the 50s. Your chances are 2½ times greater if most of the numbers are in the 50s.

Under the letter "O" there are numbers from 61 through 75. There are 9 numbers in the 60s and only 6 in the 70s. Pick a card with plenty of 60s. Your chances will be 1½ times greater.

The object is to choose cards with as many of the high-percentage numbers on them as possible.

The Full-Card Method

Most bingo games are usually won when a row is filled, but sometimes during the evening they have what are known as full-card games. In these games the player must fill in every number on his card.

In this case, the mathematical probabilities are

different. In the full-card game there are 141 numbers. There are 66 double numbers times 2 equal 132 numbers plus 9 single numbers.

Number 1 appears 17 times: 1, 10, 11, 12, 13, 14, 15, 16, 17, 18, 19, 21, 31, 41, 51, 61, 71.

Number 2 appears 17 times: 2, 12, 20, 21, 22, 23, 24, 25, 26, 27, 28, 29, 32, 42, 52, 62, 72.

Number 3 appears 17 times: 3, 13, 23, 30, 31, 32, 33, 34, 35, 36, 37, 38, 39, 43, 53, 63, 73.

Number 4 appears 17 times: 4, 14, 24, 34, 40, 41, 42, 43, 44, 45, 46, 47, 48, 49, 54, 64, 74.

Number 5 appears 17 times: 5, 15, 25, 35, 45, 50, 51, 52, 53, 54, 55, 56, 57, 58, 59, 65, 75.

Number 6 appears 16 times: 6, 16, 26, 36, 46, 56, 60, 61, 62, 63, 64, 65, 66, 67, 68, 69.

Number 7 appears 13 times: 7, 17, 27, 37, 47, 57, 67, 70, 71, 72, 73, 74, 75.

Notice that the numbers 1 through 7 appear 85 percent of the time.

Number 8 appears 7 times: 8, 18, 28, 38, 48, 58, 68.

Number 9 appears 7 times: 9, 19, 29, 39, 49, 59, 69.

Number 0 appears 7 times: 10, 20, 30, 40, 50, 60, 70.

The numbers 8, 9, and 0 appear only 15 percent of the time. When you are playing a full-card game, you should choose a card with as few 8s, 9s and 0s as possible.

If you own bingo cards, you can study these cards at home and try to figure out which rows and cards fill up more quickly. In this way you can decide which cards to choose for a professional ʒame.

There are also various computer methods for figuring out the chances of most numbers being called, but on the whole, although more reliable than other methods, they are much more complicated, and to try and apply your computerized knowledge to an actual game may not be worth the additional effort.

CONCLUSION

Millions of dollars are out there waiting for you.

Next time you get a *Reader's Digest* offer, don't throw it away. This might be the chance of a life-time. After all, you don't have to pay to enter this sweepstakes. You only have to send in the form.

The point is, you'll never win if you don't try. And there have been millions of winners, some of them even millionaire winners. You can read count-less newspaper and magazine articles about indivi-duals and families who have been able to change their lives for the better. They have been able to purchase new cars, new houses, new stereos, new carpeting. They have been able to join clubs and engage in other types of leisure activity.

In short, these people have won new lives.

You could be a lucky winner, too.

With the information in this book you are now equipped to enter a sweepstakes, a contest, or a lottery, or play bingo, with greatly increased chances of winning.

Remember, the cardinal rule is to enter often. The second cardinal rule is to follow the rules correctly.

Good-bye and good luck.